CELINE DION

FOR KEEPS

JENNA GLATZER

Andrews McMeel
Publishing

Kansas City

05 06 07 08 09 KP1 10 9 8 7 6 5 4 3 2 1

ISBN-13: 978-0-7407-5559-0

ISBN-10: 0-7407-5559-5

Library of Congress Control Number: 2005927648

Celine Dion: For Keeps is produced by
becker&mayer!, Bellevue, Washington.
www.beckermayer.com

Cover Photograph: Andre Rau

Design: Megan Noller

Editorial: Adrienne Wiley

Image Research: Shayna Ian

Production Coordination: Sheila Hackler

TABLE *of* CONTENTS

INTRODUCTION

THE LAST TIME I SAW CELINE DION, SHE WAS HEADING TO A SOUND CHECK WEARING GRAY SWEATPANTS, BOOTS, A PONYTAIL, AND WHAT LOOKED LIKE A CROSS BETWEEN WAR PAINT

and colorful clown makeup in abstract designs all over her face.

"It's my son," she explained. "He likes to be an artist. He does my makeup before I leave the house."

"But he won't let anyone paint his face," her brother Michel said. "*He's* the artist."

Celine grabbed a microphone to warm up, belting out three tunes before the show so the sound technicians could adjust their levels. She trotted around the stage in no particular pattern, chatting animatedly in French with the stage crew between verses. At one point, she lay flat on her back, continuing to sing "I'm Alive" at full power while pretending to take a nap. At another, a possibly imaginary speck of dust fell from the rafters and distracted her. She searched for it on the ground, but came up empty.

"I swear something just fell from the sky. Or it could be it was in my head. *That's it! Everything is in my head!*" she said and marched to the other side of the stage, swinging her arms exaggeratedly all the way. As soon as the music ended, she sang a little improvisational riff, then called out, "Merci beaucoup!" and ran off blowing kisses.

In thirty minutes, this woman would transform into an impeccable image of elegance. The sweat suit would be shed in favor of a corseted, breezy-skirted red dress that she says makes it impossible to breathe. The hair would be blown out and styled into flowing waves, and her son's artistic creation would be replaced by Celine's own understated but glamorous stage makeup. Tonight at the Colosseum in Las Vegas, she would meet with a dancer's family, a casino high-roller, and a fan who'd won the opportunity to meet her in a contest. Then she'd take the elevator up to the stage again and reappear to share her talent with 4,100 eager fans.

CELINE'S RISE TO INTERNATIONAL FAME DIDN'T happen overnight, and it wasn't a stroke of luck, great connections, or leather mini skirts that got her there. In a sea of pop stars who seem to dare each other to see who can generate the hottest tabloid fodder, Celine stands out as the rarest of creatures: the singer who relies purely on talent.

When I set out to write this book, I asked fans to contact me to tell me what was so special about Celine. Within one day, I heard back from everyone from twelve-year-old boys to seventy-five-year-old women from all over the United States and Canada, and from the United Kingdom, Israel, France, Russia, and beyond. About the only thing they had in common was their love for Celine and the words they used to describe what it is that is so special about her: her passion, her energy, the emotion she puts into every performance, her warmth, and the love she exudes.

Even now, after winning five Grammy Awards and selling more than 175 million albums worldwide, earning herself the title "biggest-selling female artist of all time" at the World Music Awards, she's never lost the sense of wonder and delight she felt the very first time she sang in

RIGHT: Rene-Charles prepares his mother's makeup in his own distinctive style.

front of an audience. Celine's dreams have come true many times over, and she knows full well how blessed she is.

She didn't just sit back and wait for those dreams to come true, though. With the support of her family and her manager-turned-husband, she worked to earn her career every day. And although she's no longer "building" a career, she remains one of the hardest-working women in show business, performing nearly two hundred shows annually and recording albums in English and French. In recent years, though, she's found more of the balance that previously eluded her, and it shows. The clown makeup during sound check seems a visual metaphor for the dual priorities in her life: family and music, in that order.

Although Celine may seem larger than life, the lesson she shares is a simple one: You can do whatever you set your heart on. When that twelve-year-old Quebecoise singer recorded her first demo album, she knew the odds were stacked against her ever becoming a worldwide phenomenon. She just chose to ignore the odds and plow forward, tuning out all the people who thought she was crazy along the way. In doing so, she shared a gift with the millions of listeners who have been touched by her music.

Luckily for us, she hasn't run out of dreams. If you ask her, "the best is yet to come."

ABOVE: Recording her first albums, *La Voix du Bon Dieu* and *Celine Chante Noel*, in 1981. **RIGHT:** Onstage in "A New Day . . ."

I

la P'TITE QUEBECOISE

"I always felt since I was very little that everything I owned was not

totally mine. AT A VERY YOUNG AGE, I WAS A MOTHER INSIDE.

I was giving [my playmates] my toys, and I wanted to

rock the newborn. I certainly cared for every little thing I had, and

sometimes they would break the dolls or they would take

them home, without really wanting to hurt me . . . 'She won't notice,' or

'She doesn't care; she has so many!' BUT I KNEW, AND I FELT."

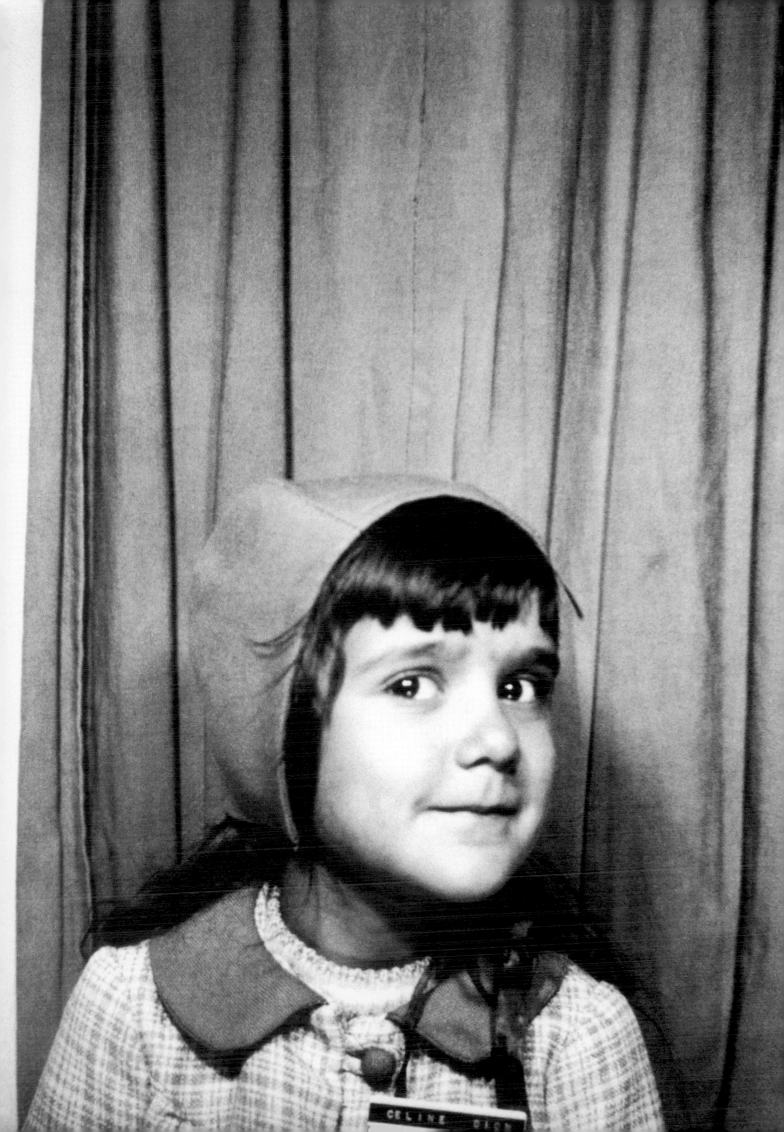

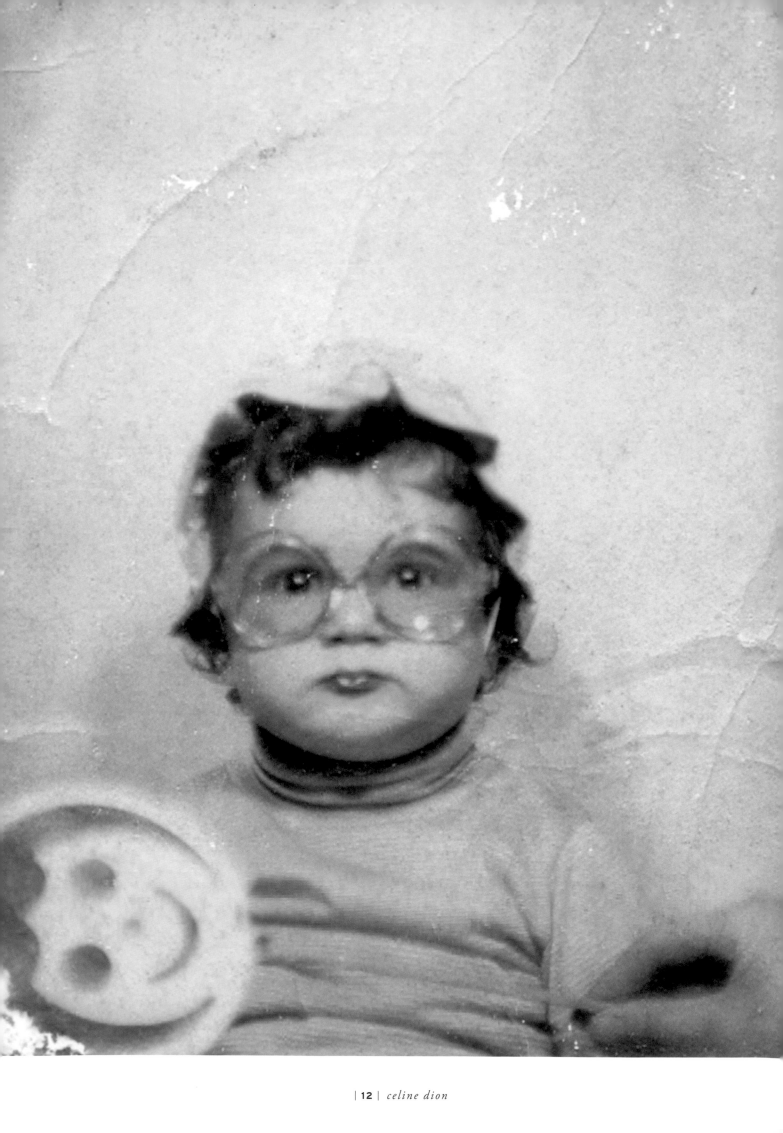

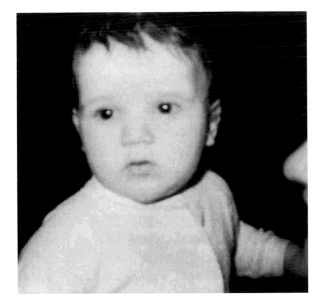

T

HERESE DION WAS NONE TOO PLEASED ABOUT BECOMING A MOTHER FOR THE FOURTEENTH TIME AT THE SAME TIME AS SHE BECAME A GRANDMOTHER. SHE HAD ASKED HER PRIEST IF

she could stop having children, but when he strongly suggested that using contraceptives was an insult to God, she listened. With eight girls and five boys, the Dion family was already far overcrowded in a small house on Notre-Dame Street in the Quebec village of Charlemagne when Therese gave birth to Celine Marie Claudette on March 30, 1968, at Le Gardeur Hospital in Repentigny.

With such an inauspicious entry into the world, it's easy to imagine that Celine might have grown up feeling deprived and unwanted, or lost in the family dynamic. On the contrary, baby Celine was like a prized toy in the household, and her siblings would fight to determine who'd get to rock the baby to sleep or give her a bath. There's a twenty-two-year age gap between Celine and her oldest sister, Denise, and a six-year gap between Celine and the two second-youngest, twins Paul and Pauline.

Celine wasn't spoiled in the way that most people use the word; there wasn't enough money to "spoil" anyone in the

family. The children literally slept in dresser drawers when they ran out of bed space—after sleeping four or five kids in each double bed. Her favorite possessions were her dolls, which she cherished as if they were real babies.

"At one point I had fourteen dolls in one big toy box," she says. "There was no way I'd let one doll have an arm on the other doll. Every one needed to breathe correctly, sleep correctly, and they needed to have a blanket."

Two of those dolls disappeared when she was young, and it's still often on her mind. Because the family saw her as young and sweet, she was expected to share everything and not complain when her toys got broken or taken. She says she was a grown-up soul, and the responsibilities she felt were out of proportion.

But Celine was certainly emotionally spoiled, soaking in all the love and attention she could possibly need from her adoring and affectionate family. Not that it resembled the Partridge Family situation so often portrayed. Therese

LEFT: An infant Celine. **ABOVE LEFT:** A star is born: Celine's first photograph. **ABOVE RIGHT:** At age two with sister Claudette, 1970. **PREVIOUS:** Circa 1973-74.

other kids. And there was just one television and one telephone in the house.

"We were watching only French television, which meant two choices of channels, so we didn't really argue about what to watch," says older brother Michel Dion. "For the telephone, only those tall enough to get the receptor could use it, because it was a wall unit five or six feet high."

Privacy, too, was tough to come by, and the older siblings were allotted special "visiting hours" when they could have a boyfriend or girlfriend over. Until 11:00 p.m. on certain days, any sibling could "claim" the living room as private space and none of the other siblings would be allowed in.

And they all shared *one* bathroom.

Adhemar took jobs as a construction worker, meat inspector, and even prison guard at a juvenile delinquent center to keep the

and Adhemar Dion were a pragmatic and inventive couple. With a family of sixteen, you can't toast bread two slices at a time in a toaster, so Therese would toss bread in the oven and toast a loaf at a time; Celine still thinks that was tastier than the fancy pastries she could afford later. Kool-Aid was cheaper than soda, so that's what the kids drank. When the family didn't have a washing machine, Therese washed all their clothes in the bathtub. It seemed that every hour of every day, laundry was being done somewhere and the clothesline in the yard was always buckled down with clothes. If someone got sick, he or she would sleep on the couch in the living room to avoid passing germs to the

kids fed and clothed, and to buy small presents for them for every birthday and Christmas, usually clothes and shoes or little toys. The whole Dion family shared the financial responsibility, too.

"There was a rule at home," Michel says. "As soon as we were able to work out of the house, we got jobs. From our paychecks, we just had to put twenty dollars per week on the table to help my parents pay their bills."

The oldest Dion child, Denise, had to quit school to work full-time. The others had a choice as to whether or not to stay in school, but Michel is the only one who graduated from high school. The various bosses of the Dion children

ABOVE: Celine and her niece Cathy, her sister Claudette's daughter. **RIGHT:** Celine at age six in 1974—the "11" indicated by the clock is surely 11:00 *p.m.*

came to dread Monday mornings. All the kids were partiers, and one was never sure who would show up after the weekend activities. Celine remembers seeing siblings coughing as they smoked and thinking, "Why do they smoke this thing that makes them choke all the time? I was very impressed they wanted to do such a thing that was making them sick, actually."

Despite the goings-on in their day-to-day lives, the family came together every day for their meals. With all sixteen people around one kitchen table, they'd tap the utensils against their glasses to make music. "If there was a note missing, we kept drinking until the water level came down to the right sound," Celine says.

Every member of the Dion family had musical talent and wanted a career in show business, and from as early as she can remember, that's all Celine ever wanted, too. She adored watching her older siblings play their instruments and practice songs in the family basement and tagging along to watch them play live gigs around Quebec. What she remembers most is the joy they got from it. They always looked so happy when they were making music, and she desperately wanted to be part of it.

Even chores were less mundane because they'd sing while they did the dishes. Therese had an excellent sense of pitch, so while the girls sang, if someone's harmony was off, she would point it out and make her correct it.

Then, after meals, Adhemar would pick up his accordion and Jacques his guitar, and each of the kids would sing a solo for the family. When Celine was a toddler, she was too short to be seen, so they'd often pop her up on the kitchen table when it was her turn, and she'd sing for hours like a wind-up toy that never seemed to wind down.

"She had all the moves, too. She'd sing love songs, all kinds of songs, the whole evening long," Michel says. He fondly remembers that she would always wait until all eyes were on her and everyone was quiet before she'd begin her private concerts. Anyone who wasn't paying attention was subject to her impatient glare.

"She had lots of talent, but I didn't say, 'Oh, she's going to be famous,' because it was natural in my family. She was like all my brothers and sisters," he says. What set her apart, though, was her complete focus and drive. Even when she was a little kid, there seemed to be nothing but music running through her mind day and night. Well, music and dressy clothes and shoes. She loved the way her sisters looked in high heels and just couldn't wait to own a pair of her own. Her clothes were mostly handmade by her mother, but she admired the models in fashion magazines and her sisters adored dressing her up like a life-sized doll. Even then, Celine was preparing for her future audience. She posed in the mirror and imagined what it would be

ABOVE LEFT: Dining out with Ghislaine, Paul, and her parents. ABOVE RIGHT: Celine with her god-parents—and siblings—Claudette and Michel. RIGHT: With sister Ghislaine.

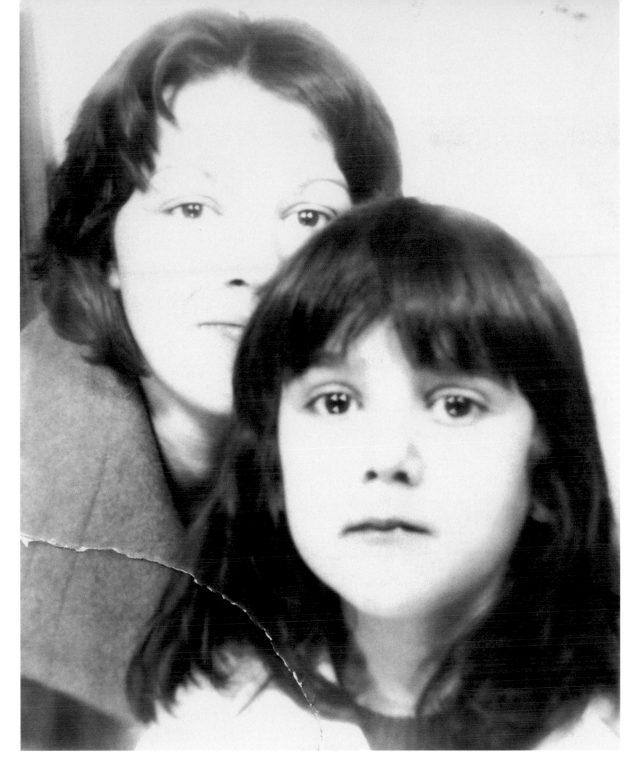

like to be a famous, glamorous singer. No one ever told her how unlikely that was to happen.

In fact, the family had their own band—A. Dion and His Ensemble. It was Adhemar's idea, which still amuses the kids, who'll quickly tell you that it was their mother who was the show business type. Although Adhemar loved music, he was prone to stage fright and was much more reserved. Therese, on the other hand, was more dramatic, talkative, and likely to yell. If one of the kids did

something wrong, she might start in on a rant of, "You get over here! How could you! Why did you! Don't you ever!" while Adhemar needed only to narrow his eyes and say, "Don't." In the band, Adhemar played the accordion, Therese the violin, and the kids took turns on various instruments and vocals. For percussion, sometimes they'd just bang against the walls if there were no drums.

"People think I grew up with classical music," says Celine. "It's not necessarily my background. I grew up with

pretty edgy music—Rush, Supertramp, Yes, Janis Joplin, the Doobie Brothers, Creedence . . ."

Little Celine's big singing debut was to come at Michel's wedding, August 18, 1973—which was also Michel's twenty-first birthday. She was five years old. "I had my own band up there, and I asked her, 'Do you want to sing a song?' She said, 'Three.' So I gave her my microphone," Michel says.

Celine remembers feeling frozen with fear just before the first note, but once she got started, she never wanted to stop. She loved the crowd's attention as much as she loved singing itself, and as she watched the guests rise to their feet in a standing ovation, her desire to perform was cemented.

In December of that year, she had her next public performance, in front of her family's coworkers. "At one point or another, almost all of Celine's family worked for my father," says Cheryl Ryshpan, whose dad owned American Salvage Store (currently known as AmSal), a clothing store in Montreal that specialized in men's work clothes. "Her sister Denise was in charge of all the gloves . . . ordering, stocking, maintaining. Her sister Liette was a super salesperson who could charm a guy who came in simply for work boots to buy a lot more." Even with fourteen kids, Celine's mom worked there, too, fixing counters because she was too shy with strangers to wait on customers.

Cheryl says, "When Celine was five, her father brought her to the staff Christmas party, along with his accordion. I will never forget that sight! Ever. Celine wore a gorgeous dress, with sparkles as I remember. Her mother had spent hours doing her hair. Her sisters kept saying, 'She'll be a star!' When she sang 'Noel,' you could hear a pin drop and there

ABOVE: The Dion family at brother Michel's wedding, August 18, 1973–the site of Celine's first public performance.

were about forty people at this staff party . . . not a cough, not a sneeze. She really made an impression."

Around 1978, Adhemar and one of the siblings, Claudette, bought a piano bar called the Vieux Baril (The Old Barrel), where the kids served as both waitstaff and entertainment. Just like at home, someone got the idea to pop Celine on top of a table, and she took off like a rocket, covering songs by her favorite French artists, Ginette Reno and Edith Piaf. Patrons came in just to see her.

At first, Therese tried to keep Celine out of the bar at nights, but she would pitch a fit. She wanted to be where her family was; she wanted to be where the action was! So they came to an agreement: As long as Celine would wake up on time for school, she was allowed to stay as late as she wanted.

The truth is that Celine didn't often make it to school on time, if she made it at all, and she spent most of her time in class daydreaming and napping—enough to concern teachers to the point of sending social workers to the home. They didn't find anything wrong with her home environment. Celine's siblings began doing her homework for her, and everyone in the family seemed to accept implicitly that singing was more important for her future than schoolwork.

Her godparents, sister Claudette and brother Michel, were two of her earliest music idols, along with sister Ghislaine. Claudette and Ghislaine often sang on stages around Quebec and on television. Michel formed a few bands—some with his siblings and some without. His best-known band was Le Show, which recorded three albums, the first in 1978. They even made television specials, had a chart-topping hit, and received many award nominations in Quebec.

ABOVE: Holding a hat at Michel's wedding. BOTTOM: With Michel at his wedding.

He recalls his first family band tour: "Jacques was a guitarist with no guitar; Daniel was the drummer, but no drums; Ghislaine was the keyboard player and singer . . . no keyboard. So I bought instruments for everyone. I went to the bank for a $12,000 loan, then we bought brand-new instruments and an old school bus. We'd go on the road, find a bar, stop there and say, 'Sir, need a band? We're a band.'" For three years, they played at a formerly struggling bar that was usually near empty; within three months of the band's arrival, the doorman had to lock people out when it got too crowded on weekends.

Celine couldn't imagine anything better than what her successful siblings were doing. She was miserable when they went touring too far for her to follow and couldn't wait to be among them. But she had the Vieux Baril, and its patrons had become just as addicted to Celine as she had to their applause and approval. Then the bar burned down in 1981. Of course it was a disaster for all the family, but Celine was devastated. Where would she perform now?

How about . . . everywhere?

AT TWELVE YEARS OLD, ABOUT THE SAME TIME that she was expected to find her first job, Celine told her mother that she wanted a career in singing. Working part-time stocking shelves in a clothing store would just delay her dreams. All Therese wanted to know was if Celine was serious. She was ready to put all her energy into making Celine a star, and once she had the reassurance that her daughter was committed, she vowed to make it happen.

Therese went to American Salvage in tears, explaining that she had to quit her job, but everyone understood quite well that Maman Dion was about to start a much more important job. She was going to coach Celine, to be there for her every step of the way. Therese's life now had a laser-beam focus: making her daughter a professional singer.

To help Celine gain experience, Therese signed her up for local singing contests and brought her to sing at parties and community fairs. Briefly, Celine had a manager who wanted

ABOVE: Celine working on her homework at age thirteen—probably a publicity shot, if she looks that happy about studying. RIGHT: The Dion family gathers as A. Dion and His Ensemble.

"SHE HAD LOTS OF TALENT, BUT I DIDN'T SAY, 'OH, SHE'S
GOING TO BE FAMOUS,' BECAUSE IT WAS NATURAL IN MY FAMILY. SHE
WAS LIKE ALL MY BROTHERS AND SISTERS." —MICHEL DION

her to record a demo, but he didn't know any songwriters who could write appropriate songs for a preteen balladeer. After all, edgy rock songs and passionate love songs just wouldn't cut it with Celine—a young girl who loved dolls and had a crush on hockey player Gilbert Delorme.

Therese decided that if she wanted the job done right, she'd do it herself, so she set to work writing a song just for Celine. "Ce N'etait Qu'un Reve (It Was Only A Dream)" was the product of her lyrics and sketch of a melody, and brother Jacques's arrangement, with Celine adding her own variation on the melody of the bridge. At a recording studio, Celine made a demo tape of the song, along with Therese's second composition "Grand-maman (Grandmother)" and a remake of the Jean Lapointe song "Chante-la Ta Chanson (Sing Your Song)."

Rene Angelil had been a member of the Baronets, Quebec's answer to the Beatles, and was then a manager and producer. After finding Rene's name and address on a Ginette Reno album, Therese wrapped the demo tape in a red bow and had Michel drive her to drop it off at Rene's office. Then she waited. And waited.

What they didn't know was that Rene was about to quit show business after a falling out with Ginette, his star singer. "Ginette kept telling me not to talk to her in front of her boyfriend about business because he didn't know anything about show business, and every time I left he would say the contrary of what I said. He was envious—he wanted to be part of the business. So I stopped talking about it in front of him," Rene says. A year later, Ginette told Rene she wanted her boyfriend to comanage her career. Rene walked away in disappointment and financial ruin. Loyalty is a trait he prizes, and to have his trust broken this way stole his desire to work with other artists.

Maybe a more reliable career was in order, he decided. Before he entered show business, he had begun law school.

THE BARONETS

PERSONAL MANAGEMENT
BEN KAYE
MONTREAL, CANADA

He and his second wife, Anne-Renee, discussed it and decided that Rene would go back and finish the two years of school it would take for him to earn a law degree. But there was a sadness in that decision, a defeat that Rene had trouble accepting. "Here I am leaving show business, the business I had been in for twenty years as an artist, a manager, producer, and I have to leave because she's stupid, and this guy, too," he says.

A week after he made the decision to quit, he got the now-famous call from Celine's brother Michel, who was tired of watching his mother sit around the house waiting for the phone to ring. "I know you didn't listen to the tape of my sister, because if you did, you would have called us," Michel said. The tape was sitting around Rene's office, and he reluctantly stuck it in the tape player, mostly to appease Michel. Hundreds of mothers had sent him tapes like this, and every one was convinced that her little darling was the next big thing. That's why it shocked him when he realized Michel wasn't lying. What he heard coming out of those speakers delighted him. Could it be that his star client had walked out of his life just in time for him to discover an even bigger star? He had to see for himself if this little girl was the real thing, so he called and arranged a meeting.

When she walked into his office, Celine was overwhelmed by this handsome man in a suit and tie with all his gold records on the wall. He even had his own assistant. To her,

he looked like the embodiment of what she dreamed about: "big-time" success. Her crush on him was instantaneous.

"She wasn't a cute little girl, by the way, at twelve years old," says Rene. "She grew up very fast around fourteen years old, but at twelve she was very small, and she had bad teeth She didn't smile a lot because of her bad teeth. She wasn't saying a word; her mother was doing the talking. She wasn't the kind of girl where you say, 'Oh, isn't she cute, won't she be great on TV?' Not at all."

That was a blow to Rene's hopes, but he still wanted to hear what she could do. He asked her to stand up and sing as if she were in the biggest theatre in Montreal. Celine hesitated for a moment until Therese explained that Celine always sang with a microphone. Rene handed her a pen and told her to pretend. Suddenly, the mousy little girl transformed before his eyes. She looked off as if she were envisioning the balcony and the great audience of people who had come to listen to her, a visualization she had practiced a thousand times in the mirror at home. With emotion and presence that belied her age, she exploded into song . . . suddenly, her less-than-perfect appearance and shyness faded into an afterthought.

"What excited me was her incredible voice, and only the voice," Rene says. And what excited Celine and her mom was that they saw Rene tear up with emotion as Celine sang. He signed her on as his only client on the spot.

ABOVE: Advertisement for Celine's performance at a local event. **LEFT:** Rene (right) was part of the popular Quebec group The Baronets, with Pierre Labelle and Jean Beaulne.

NOTE FROM EDDY MARNAY AND MIA DUMONT

Hired by Rene to write songs for his new client, Eddy Marnay soon became one of Celine's early professional confidants, as did his companion, Mia Dumont, who became Celine's publicist. Eddy's songs both were age-appropriate for Celine and helped her learn about life from their words. Those songs formed the core of two of her first albums, *La Voix du Bon Dieu (The Voice of God)*, a phrase Eddy had coined on first hearing her sing, and *Tellement J'ai D'amour* . . . . Celine became close to both Eddy and Mia, and was crushed when she had to begin working with other songwriters until they met with Eddy's approval.

Eddy and Mia sent this note to Celine on the occasion of her premiere at the Olympia opening for Patrick Sebastien. It reads: "Wishing you the power to hold the note for two hundred years to come. We embrace you."

REPORT CARD FROM STE-MARIE-DES-ANGES ELEMENTARY SCHOOL

Celine was never a dedicated student, preferring instead to stay up late singing with the family. This is the report card for the school year that ended in summer 1977, when Celine was nine years old. Over that year, she earned an average of a B in social sciences, a C in natural sciences, and a 67 percent in mathematics (her classmates averaged an 80). Nor did she fare much better in her communication classes, in which she averaged a B in speaking, a C in listening, a 62 percent in reading (versus the class average of 75), and a 57 percent in writing (the class reached an average of 77). Ever the dancer, however, she averaged an A in physical education.

LEAD SHEET FOR "CE N'ETAIT QU'UN REVE"

When Therese Dion took on the task of making her daughter a star, she began by looking for the perfect song for Celine's demo tape. There was nothing quite right for the then twelve-year-old, so Therese worked with Celine's brother Jacques to write "Ce N'etait Qu'un Reve (It Was Only A Dream)." After Celine recorded the song at a studio, one copy of that demo tape found its way to Rene's desk. And the rest, as they say, is history.

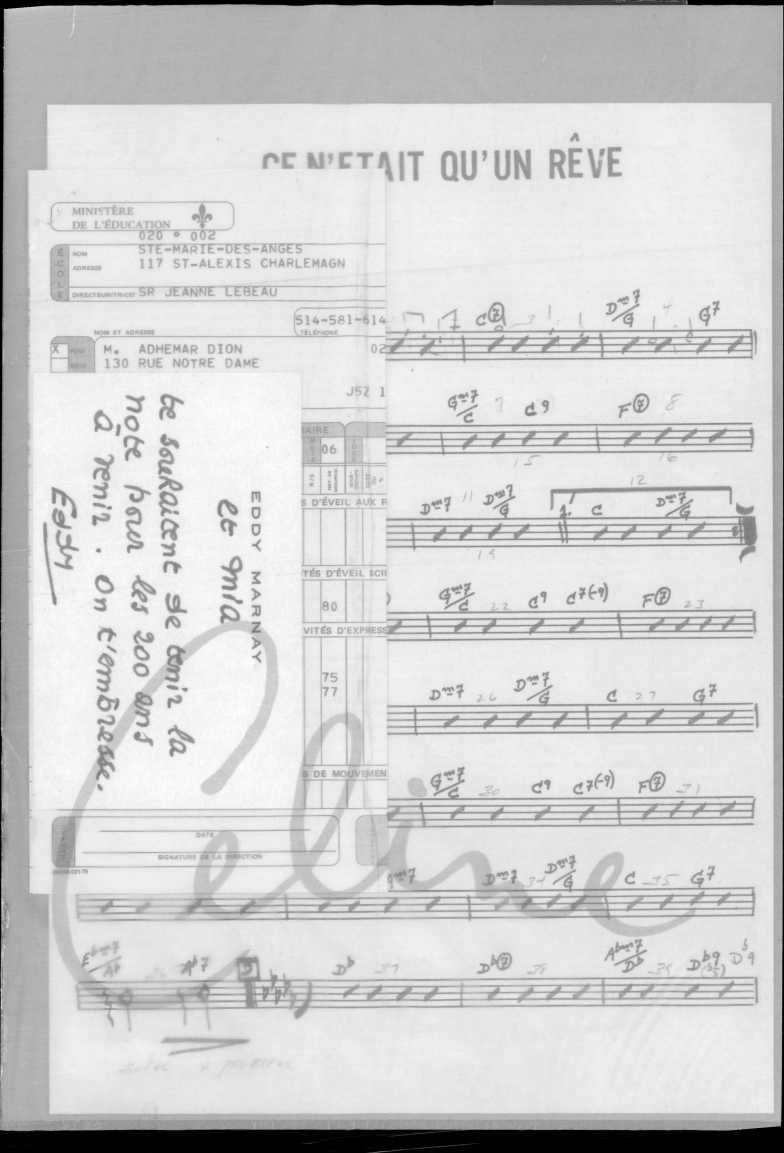

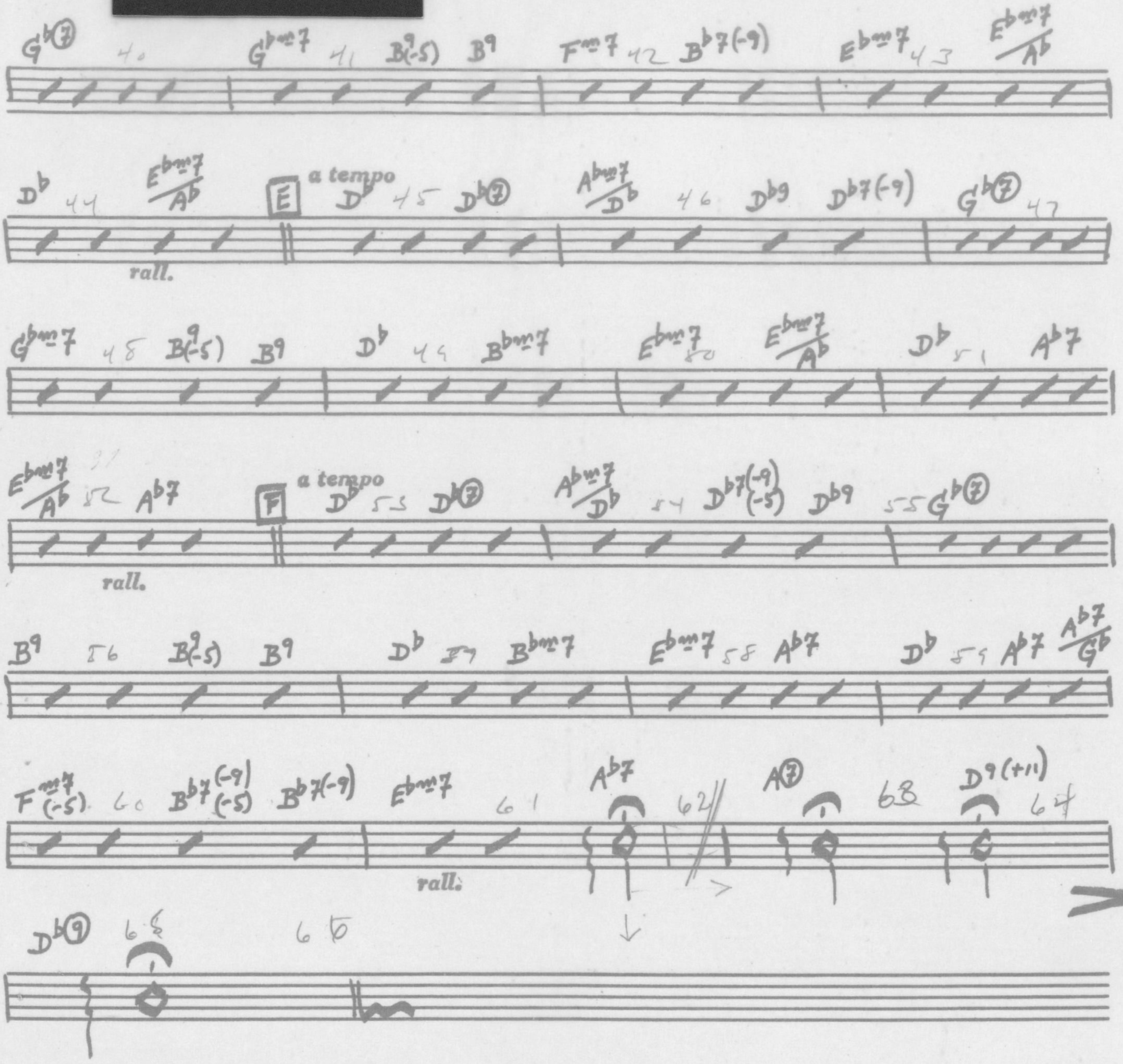

Copiste :

MARCEL LEVEQUE

Céline Dion

"Une voix d'or
dans un cœur d'enfant "

ce n'était qu'un rêve

l'amour viendra

Right away, Rene went about the business of trying to get other people as excited about Celine's potential as he was. He didn't expect her to become an international sensation. ("I'm not a genius," he says.) After all, she couldn't even speak English—a requirement for global appeal. But he did believe she could have a very successful career in Quebec and France, and he told her mother that he'd make her a star within five years.

Rene had a plan. She would record two albums back-to-back: one album of ballads and another of Christmas songs. "In Quebec, Christmas albums have even a bigger effect than in the United States. I figured if we put out two albums at the same time, people in the business would say, 'I'd better give it a listen.' It would get their attention."

Unfortunately, none of the record executives agreed. "They were all saying, 'Yes, it's true the little girl has a great voice, but we want to start with a single and see how it goes.' I definitely wanted to put her out with two albums," he says.

So Rene took the biggest risk of his life: With his wife's approval, he mortgaged his home for $80,000 to start his own record company just to produce Celine's first records. Rene's friends thought he was crazy to bet so much on an awkward twelve-year-old girl, but he remained determined.

"It was my last chance," he says, and he was going to make the most of this chance. He knew he had to gain the full support and trust of Celine's family, especially her parents, to make this bet pay off. He had a lot of respect for his own parents, so he wanted to prove to the Dions that he had the right intentions. He made frequent visits to their house to get to know them better. Right away, he hit it off with Celine's father, Adhemar.

"He had confidence in me because I was a very well-known artist in Quebec," Rene says. "The family had followed my career with the Baronets. He never voiced an opinion about career strategy, but he was completely supportive."

Celine says Rene became part of the family right away. "We all trusted him because he's very lovable and very smart. They were all impressed because he was very truthful—no bullshit. I'm the baby of the family, and there were a lot of eyes on him. But there are only good things in his heart. He never would've thought of making money off my back."

Then Rene set out to find a perfect songwriter. When he had tried to get a record deal for Ginette Reno in France, Rene kept hearing that he should work with the great Algerian-born French songwriter Eddy Marnay. Eddy wrote more than three thousand songs in his career, mostly for French artists like Nana Mouskouri, Claude Francois, and Edith Piaf, but also for some international artists, including Barbra Streisand. Eddy was the first person Rene thought of for Celine, and he proved to be the right choice. Upon hearing Celine sing for the first time, Eddy exclaimed that Celine had "the voice of God."

And better yet, Eddy's companion, Mia Dumont, was already a publicist and press agent to great French and Canadian artists. She was hired to introduce Celine to Quebec's media and get them to look past her less-than-adorable appearance. Celine bonded with both Eddy and Mia immediately, and they spent a great deal of time just getting to know her. Eddy wanted to write songs that Celine would relate to, so he chatted with her about everything that was important to her. Despite a forty-five-year age gap between them, Eddy was easily able to tap into Celine's feelings and talk on her level.

ABOVE: Celine with Eddy Marnay, Mia Dumont, and Rene at the l'ADISQ awards, 1983. **RIGHT:** At her first meeting with the famous songwriter—and soon her close friend—Eddy Marnay.

"IT WAS A BIG BLESSING FOR ME TO HAVE EDDY MARNAY WRITING THOSE LYRICS FOR ME AT THAT

AGE. IT'S NOT EASY TO WRITE FOR A TWELVE- OR THIRTEEN-YEAR-OLD, FINDING INTERESTING

THINGS TO TALK ABOUT—NOT ABOUT APPLES AND PEARS AND MY MOM AND MY DADDY....I LEARNED

FROM MY SONGS ABOUT LIFE, ABOUT REALITY, AND LOVE AS WELL." –CELINE

"It was a big blessing for me to have Eddy Marnay writing those lyrics for me at that age," says Celine. "It's not easy to write for a twelve- or thirteen-year-old, finding interesting things to talk about—not about apples and pears and my mom and my daddy. He always found interesting ways for me to grow and learn through my songs. I didn't go to school for a long time and I learned from my songs about life, about reality, and love as well."

Once they had a demo tape with Eddy's songs, Rene called the host of Quebec's most popular talk show, Michel Jasmin, and asked him to come to his office to hear it.

Although there was no full album yet, Michel agreed to introduce Celine to the public. On June 19, 1981, she made her television debut on his show, and she was terrified. The nerves had nothing to do with her singing, but everything to do with the interview. What would he ask her? What was she supposed to say? Rene reassured her that she would know the answers to anything he asked. "He'll ask how many brothers and sisters you have and you'll say

thirteen, and he'll ask where you're from and you'll say Repentigny," Rene instructed. Except that Celine lived in Charlemagne.

"When he said the name of the town, he gave me the wrong town without noticing. I was listening to him so well that when the guy asked me, 'Where are you from?,' I said Repentigny. I don't know if it's innocence or believing in the person who shows you the way or it's totally stupid, wanting to succeed so much. I didn't mean to lie about my hometown. I was just listening to my manager. The beginning of my career went fast. Even though inside I felt strong, I was so young. I was so fragile."

The song went off beautifully, but she was later embarrassed by most of her interview answers—for example, Jasmin had asked her if she wanted to take singing lessons, and Celine appeared annoyed before dismissing him with a quick, "No."

The audience didn't mind, though, and Celine quickly earned the affectionate nickname "la p'tite Quebecoise" (little Quebecker).

ABOVE: With disc jockey Robert Arcand and her first albums, *La Voix du Bon Dieu* and *Celine Chante Noel*. **LEFT TOP:** Eddy Marnay, Celine, Therese Dion, and Rene. **LEFT BOTTOM:** With Michel Jasmin and Pierre Lalonde on Jasmin's popular talk show.

In October 1981 they released two albums: *La Voix du Bon Dieu (The Voice of God)* and *Celine Chante Noel (Celine Sings Christmas)*. Then, Rene launched Celine's first tour—a tour of shopping malls around Quebec. Every winter, the malls would either hire Santa Claus or a performer to appear on a stage slightly larger than a dinner table . . . and during her first tour, Celine wished she were Santa Claus instead of a little-known singer.

"We were promoting albums, arranging a meeting for the record store to have a lot of records and a little desk, knowing that after I sang I would sign autographs. It was awful. I love to sing, but most of the time, probably every

time, it was early afternoon. I'm a night bird. For me, the darker it is outside the better it is. It was so early that it felt like I wasn't really in my clothes yet, my voice was not warmed up, my makeup was out to here . . . " she says, putting her hand several inches in front of her face.

"I wanted to be a big star. This was not at the level of a big star in my head. We wished for a lot of people surrounding that stage that I sing to: *Oh di hop, oh di hop, oh di hop, ohe!* ["Giddyup, giddyup, giddyup, let's go" from the French version of "Winter Wonderland"] . . . Oh, no. People were walking by and saying, 'Oh, isn't she sweet?,' then moving along and going shopping! They didn't know me. It was so

ABOVE: By her second Christmas on the mall circuit, Celine was mobbed by fans. **RIGHT:** At the shopping mall with Santa Claus, the Star Fairy, and Rene.

hard. I never questioned what my manager was asking me to do. I trusted him with my eyes closed and my heart open, but I didn't like doing that."

By the first Christmas, the two albums had sold more than 30,000 copies. They'd go on to sell about 125,000 copies by the following year. It didn't quite pay off Rene's mortgage, but it certainly helped him make payments to get rid of his debt.

Little by little, the singer was making her mark. As she became a public figure, the media was quick to make fun of Celine's long, pointed incisor teeth, just like her classmates, who often called her "Dracula." One humor magazine even dubbed her "Canine Dion," which led her to angle her face upward when she spoke and to hide her mouth with the microphone when she could. But overall, the media in Quebec was kind. They also called her "the next Judy Garland," and before long, Celine's name was all over newspapers and magazines. The next time she toured, things were different on the mall circuit.

"Now it was a free-for-all. Some people were stealing in stores while I was performing because everybody was surrounding the stage looking at me, even the salesmen in the boutiques. They were looking at me while people were thieves! There were so many people that I couldn't perform in shopping malls anymore. I was very proud. I was Santa Claus!"

Celine told Rene that all she wanted to do was sing; he could handle all the other details. "I didn't want to handle anything other than singing because to do it right is difficult," she says. "Singing is a big discipline. Every kind of work is a lot of discipline, if you want to do it right. Singing is technically hard, vocally hard, it's muscles—you have to protect them, you have to train them. You can't train them too much, but just enough. I was very young then; I wanted to enjoy myself, and I wanted to sing. I didn't want to try to figure out or hear about the business aspect of it. I think that's why I'm still healthy today. I think it protected me."

Rene was glad to have a singer who trusted him so implicitly, and he quickly learned the right buttons to push to get Celine to do her best: He just had to put the pressure on. The more he made it sound like a particular performance was her "big shot," the better she would perform. He sometimes exaggerated the risks, telling her that if she blew it this time,

TOP: At the Tokyo subway with fans, 1982. **BOTTOM LEFT:** Celine with the other gold medalist and another participant at the World Popular Song Festival. **BOTTOM RIGHT:** Celine poses with Rene after her performance in Tokyo.

NOV. - 1. 1982
1982 WORLD POPULAR SONG FESTIVAL IN TOKYO

Breakfast   ¥ 1,500   (No refund)

ROOM   NO._____

SIGNATURE_____

Hotel Grand Palace

she'd lose her shot at ever making it big. That just seemed to add to her determination. She was in a constant contest with herself, always out to reach new heights and perform better than the last time.

In 1972 Ginette Reno had won the Yamaha World Popular Song Festival in Tokyo, a prestigious competition that ran annually from 1970 to 1989. Now, a decade later, Rene wanted to show off his protégée.

This would be her biggest performance yet, and the first time she'd sing in front of an international audience. Because her songwriter, Eddy Marnay, was French, she represented France—a bit ironic because the French music industry hadn't yet warmed up to her.

Celine was thrilled but also anxious. "I remember very much the spaghetti bolognese in Japan, because I couldn't eat anything else. I was only having spaghetti bolognese or hamburger steak," she says. "We had coupons because we were participants of the contest. And the artists who were being eliminated gave us their coupons, so we could eat so much!"

On her way to the stage as the fifth contestant to perform, she found a five-yen coin from 1968—the year of her birth—and stuck it in her shoe; this was to become her good luck charm. Celine tied with a Mexican singer for the gold medal for "Best Song with Tellement J'ai D'amour Pour Toi" and won the special orchestra award outright.

"I think it was 100 million people watching, and performing with a huge orchestra was wonderful. I couldn't afford that kind of orchestra," she says. "I had a great time: the food, the hotel, the foreign country, my mom being there, meeting new people, and bicycles . . . hundreds and hundreds of bicycles on the street . . . this is what I remember more than the gold medal. I didn't need a medal to show I won. I sang the best I could."

Her homecoming was outrageous. Quebec treated Celine like royalty. They were so proud of their little star for her victory, even coming out to the airport by the hundreds to congratulate her when she landed back in her home country. Even the Premier of Quebec, Rene Levesque, visited to welcome her home. But Celine's impression was that her fans were happier than she was about her "big win."

"I was more proud for the people in Quebec than for me. If I didn't win, I'm sure they would've been at the airport supporting me anyway," she says. "It made a difference for them, really. It did not for me. And I don't mean that in a

ABOVE: One of the many dining coupons Celine collected from other singers as they were eliminated from the Song Festival.

negative way—I'm not saying it didn't matter. But I didn't feel any difference for me to win whenever I wanted my career, or how much money I made on the record deal, but it impresses the people in the business and it impresses the fans and people in the place you're from. It's like they want to dream. They want happiness, they want success, they want to see the gold, they want to see the champions. They don't want to see the struggle, the negative, the losers, the second best." Celine believes fans love seeing a "regular person" make it big.

The next year, in 1983, Celine won four of Quebec's Felix Awards for Best New Artist, Best Album (*Tellement J'ai D'amour . . .*), Best Female Artist, and Best Performance Outside the Province of Quebec.

Then came an astounding invitation: Pope John Paul II was visiting Quebec in 1984, and she was asked to perform for him to represent the children of Quebec. In Montreal's Olympic stadium, she sang "Une Colombe (A Dove)" from the album *Melanie* in front of 65,000 people. "It was such a big thing for me—it felt as much as if I were going to meet God," she says. "Does this mean that something miraculous would happen? It got my curiosity tremendously. I thought, 'This is as close to Heaven as I'm going to be during life.' It was intimidating."

Shortly after that, Celine was invited to Italy with her mother and Rene to have a private session with Pope John Paul II. "He spoke to us in French, and he was so charismatic. Then Rene told him my mother had fourteen children, and I said to myself, 'Did you have to tell him that? Do you think he cares? Maybe he's seen better than that. Maybe it's a big deal for us, not for him.' But then he said to my mother that he was blessing the whole family." The experience left all three of them in tears and awed Celine's already growing fan base. When they came back to Montreal, journalists couldn't stop asking about her meeting with the pope.

By 1985, Celine had recorded five albums, and Rene felt it was time for her first true tour, on which she performed thirty-six shows in twenty-five Quebec cities. Although she had no idea what the lyrics meant, they added a few English songs to the tour, including "What A Feeling," "Up Where We Belong," and "Over The Rainbow." Her first live album, which

ABOVE AND RIGHT: Celine, Rene, and Therese met with Pope John Paul II at the Vatican in October 1985.

"IT WAS SUCH A BIG THING FOR ME—IT FELT AS MUCH AS IF I WERE GOING TO MEET GOD. DOES THIS MEAN SOMETHING MIRACULOUS WOULD HAPPEN? . . . I THOUGHT, 'THIS IS AS CLOSE TO HEAVEN AS I'M GOING TO BE DURING LIFE.'" —CELINE

TBS

MONTREAL, LE 10 JUILLET 1984

DIRECTION DEPARTEMENTALE DE LA
MAIN D'OEUVRE DE PARIS
2 bis, rue de Jussiène
BUREAU 102

75002 - PARIS

A L'ATTENTION DE MADAME HYEST

Monsieur le Directeur Départemental,

Nous nous proposons de produire sur la scène de l'Olympia CELINE DION qui présentera son spectacle lors du passage de PATRICK SEBASTIEN du 06 Novembre au 09 Décembre 1984.

Nous vous remercions de bien vouloir lui accorder le permis de travail règlementaire ainsi qu'à son musicien.

Pour ce faire, vous trouverez en annexe, tous les renseignements les concernant.

Vous remerciant par avance,

Veuillez agréer, Monsieur le Directeur Départemental, l'expression de mes sentiments distingués.

René Angelil

René ANGELIL

- Merci de faire parvenir l'autorisation de travail au Théâtre de l'Olympia.

LES PRODUCTIONS TBS INC. 1600, BOUL. LE CORBUSIER, SUITE 202, LAVAL, QUÉBEC, CANADA H7S 1Y9 TÉL.: (514) 687-1851

came out in December of that year, was recorded at a sold-out performance at Place des Arts in Montreal. Her singing was roundly applauded, but her patter was criticized greatly.

"I had to learn everything by heart if I needed to talk to a crowd onstage," she says. "People were criticizing me because what came out of my mouth was not natural. Of course not. 'It looks like she learned everything.' You are so right. I learned by heart. Why? Because I didn't have a life before, and I didn't know how to talk to an audience."

Beyond that, she was also afraid of writing anything other than her autograph. When she was asked to write a message to someone, she would whisper to Rene to ask him what to write and how to spell it. She still remembers the pressure once of being asked to sign a message on a giant wall. If she made a mistake, it would be permanently showcased there.

"You have to remember," she says, "I dropped out of school in the tenth grade." This is something she's still self-conscious of today. Journalists who have more formal education than she has can intimidate her, and she sometimes feels tense about "sounding smart" when they ask about subjects other than her music. But it concerned her more then, when she was first trying to get taken seriously in her field.

Celine had her heart set so thoroughly on having a major career that she catastrophized every time something went wrong, like when she got sick and her voice wasn't at its best, or when she felt she sounded foolish in an interview. Sometimes she looks back on how much weight was on her shoulders during these early teen years and says she wouldn't go through it again—instead, "I should have stayed at home and had fourteen kids!"

But then she smiles. As stressful as the journey was, it's what led her to where she is today. A place where she's still learning about who she really is and what fulfills her. A place where she's growing more comfortable with being imperfect and human but still beautiful. And maybe a place where that determined little child can finally begin to play.

ABOVE: Celine opens for Patrick Sebastien at the Olympia in Paris in late 1984, part of a month-and-a-half stint touring with him in France. LEFT: Rene's request for a French work permit for Celine during the Patrick Sebastien tour (see translation, page 190).

TOUR SCHEDULE WITH PATRICK SEBASTIEN

One of Celine's early running gigs was opening for comedian Patrick Sebastien in Paris in late 1984.

The letter to Rene from Sebastien's manager reads:

Dear Sir,

As discussed when we talked previously, I hereby confirm the presence of Celine Dion:

1. Patrick Sebastien Tour, October 25th to 31st, 1984, in the following cities:
- 25th, Moulin
- 26th, Macon
- 27th, Annecy
- 29th, Anger
- 30th, Chartres
- 31st, Corbeil

2. Olympia, From November 6th to December 9th, 1984

We agreed to an artistic fee of 3,500.00 French francs for each performance, for the tour as well as for the Olympia.

I will make sure that the rehearsals with the orchestra will be on October 22nd and 23rd, 1984. Celine Dion will also participate in Michel Drucker's television show of October 20th, 1984, rehearsal on the 19th.

I hope this message finds you well,

Sincerely yours,
Jacques Marouani

MAROUANI ORGANISATION

Monsieur René ANGELIL
LES PRODUCTIONS TBS INC.,
9255 Joseph Mélançon
MONTREAL
QUEBEC H2M 2H6

Paris,
Le 16 Mai
1984

Monsieur,

Pour faire suite à notre entretien, je vous confirme
par la présente la participation de Céline DION :

1) - _Tournée de Patrick SEBASTIEN_

   du 25 au 31 Octobre 1984 dans les villes suivantes :

      - Le 25 MOULIN
      - Le 26 MACON
      - Le 27 ANNECY
      - Le 29 ANGER
      - Le 30 CHARTRES
      - Le 31 CORBEIL

2) - _OLYMPIA_

   du 6 Novembre au 9 Décembre 1984

Nous nous sommes mis d'accord sur un cachet de 3.500,00 F TTC
par réprésentation, aussi bien pour la tournée d'octobre
que pour l'Olympia.

Par ailleurs, je ferais le nécessaire pour que les
répétitions avec l'orchestre aient lieu le 22 et 23
Octobre 1984, Céline DION pourra également participer
à l'émission de Michel DRUCKER prévue le 20 Octobre 1984
avec répétition le 19.

Vous souhaitant bonne réception de la présente,

Veuillez agréer, Monsieur, l'expression de mes
sentiments dévoués.

Jacques MAROUANI

35, RUE MARBEUF, 75008 PARIS - TEL. 225.65.90 - CABLES, MAROUANI PARIS - TELEX, 643 319 F
EN AUCUN CAS, LES OFFRES CONTENUES DANS CETTE LETTRE NE POURRONT TENIR LIEU D'ENGAGEMENT. R.C. PARIS A 72I075844 LICENCE N° 285

THE POWER *of* THE DREAM

"The thing that I'm the MOST PROUD of is

not my bank account, not my gold records or my awards.

It's what we have achieved IN FRIENDSHIP,

AS LOVERS, AS HUSBAND AND WIFE, AS FAMILY,

grounded from day one to today."

L'actualité

15 JUIN 1993 / 2,50 $

DION-ANGÉLIL
Un duo d'enfer

Il parie, elle chante, ils gagnent !

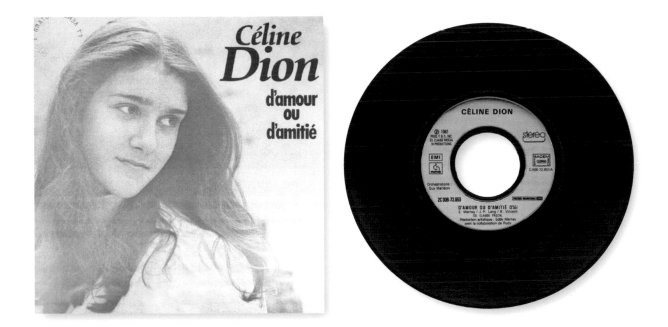

WHEN SHE TALKS ABOUT HER CAREER, CELINE NEVER USES THE WORD "I." IT'S ALWAYS "WE." "WE HAD GOALS," SHE SAYS. "WE WANTED TO HAVE SUCCESS,

but more than success, we wanted to realize our dream, which was to be in show business forever. We wanted to sing, we wanted to do the biggest TV shows, and we wanted to come to America. I wanted to be on the same stage as the people we were admiring."

Even when she was a teen, she thought of Rene as her teammate. They shared the same visions. She told him her dreams and left it up to him to coordinate how she would achieve them. "I wanted to have an international career. He felt that for a little girl I was thinking big, and he loved that because he was thinking big, too, but making it happen is hard."

Rene's plan was to get Celine seen by all the right people, to put her in spots where decision-makers would get to see her live onstage. This was where she shone brightest; it was one thing to hear her voice on the radio, but another thing entirely to see the little body it emanated from, to fall under the spell of this girl whose passion was infectious.

"So many things we've done without making money," Celine recalls. "My mother and I, we were questioning ourselves sometimes—'Why is he asking us to do this that pays nothing instead of this that pays a lot?' Well, he knew what was smarter for my career. We didn't doubt him, but we asked ourselves questions because we needed money to survive. Rene always worked like, 'If I had $1 million in my pocket right now, would I ask Celine to do this?' Most of the time the answer was no. So we didn't make money for a long time."

Not that anyone realized that. "People thought we were rich people, thought that we were big-time, because we were pretending we were *it*—big thing, big time," she says. She learned to act as if she had already made it, to exude the kind of confidence that makes other people assume success is inevitable.

In 1983 Celine became the first Canadian to earn a gold record in France when her single "D'amour Ou D'amitie (Love Or Friendship)" sold more than 700,000 copies. But France wasn't hooked on Celine yet. It was difficult to get her

---

ABOVE: Cover and record of the best-selling single *D'amour Ou D'amitie*. **LEFT:** The cover of Quebec's *L'actualite* from 1993 says it all: "A hell of a team: He gambles, she sings, they win!" **PREVIOUS:** Rene and Celine at a press conference in her early years as a performer.

any radio play there, and it seemed her age and ultrasweet image were working against her.

While watching the American Music Awards on television with her family and Rene in 1985, she became enthralled with Michael Jackson. Even though she couldn't understand his language, she loved his stage presence. The longer they watched the show, the more excited she got about the prospect of one day performing alongside the biggest American artists. "I can see myself like that," she told Rene.

"Then we have to make a deal," he said. "If you're going to make a splash in America, we should stop right away, and you need to go back to school to learn how to speak English. Then I'll get you a contract with a record company."

She agreed and thus began an eighteen-month hiatus. Not only would she learn English, but she'd lose her childish image. Rene wanted there to be a definitive break where the public wouldn't get to see the transformation taking place behind the scenes. They wouldn't see her again as a child; in those eighteen months, he hoped the public would forget her old image and get ready to accept a new one. The timing was right for him, too; his marriage to Anne-Renee was falling apart, and he needed time to attend to his own life.

He enrolled Celine in the Berlitz School, where she studied five days a week, nine hours a day, for two months. There, she had to speak English all the time in sort of a trial by fire. It frustrated her at first, but she soon became a better student than she ever was before.

Then her main order of business was to change her look. Her teeth would be capped and she'd get braces, her hair would be cut, and she'd toss away the high-necked Sunday school dresses in favor of sexier clothes and makeup. A dream come true for Celine!

During the hiatus, Rene visited Las Vegas with two of his best friends, Marc Verreault and Ben Kaye. The trio attended Wayne Newton's Elvis tribute concert at the Hilton. Rene was a huge fan of Elvis and also a huge fan of his manager, Colonel Parker.

After the concert, for five dollars, audience members could visit Elvis's old suite and buy souvenirs. Ben spotted

The Colonel in the suite and immediately ran over to tell him about Rene and what a big fan he was. "Ben was a pushy guy—he used to be a manager himself, our band's manager," says Rene. "He knew that The Colonel was one of my idols, so he went to see him and said, 'This guy with me manages a young singer. Would you mind if I take a picture of you with him?'"

But he didn't stop at one picture, embarrassing Rene to no end. Finally, The Colonel asked about this girl Rene managed. What kind of music did she sing? Rene said that her style was like Barbra Streisand's.

"Let me give you some advice," said The Colonel. "When you talk about your artist, never mention another artist. First of all, Barbra Streisand is a close friend of mine. She'll never be Barbra Streisand; you know that. And it only diminishes the artist to compare her."

Rene took his advice to heart, vowing never to compare Celine to anyone when he pitched her. It didn't take long to prove his vow. Rene was awed by Celine's change in appearance, and although he didn't realize how well she'd already mastered the language, he agreed to let her try to do an interview in English. Shocked by the way she understood questions and spoke with ease, he set out to get her a major record contract.

He approached CBS Records (soon to be bought out by Sony). CBS was confused at first. After all, Rene was making a lot of money releasing her albums himself rather than sharing profits with a record company. But Rene had never wanted to be a record executive. His label was a small company in Quebec with no international presence. He had intended it to be a starting platform for Celine, nothing more. "My main goal was to think of the artist. What was best for her, to be in my record company or to be with CBS? Obviously, it's to be with CBS and have a chance to grow," he says.

When CBS executive producer Vito Luprano heard Celine at a private party, he was blown away. Then he met with Rene and felt like they had been friends forever. "Many times in this business, it's about who's trying to impress who. People are insecure and always trying to prove themselves, where with Rene, it was a magical moment for me," says

ABOVE: Celine with one of her Berlitz English tutors, Linda McEwen, critical in her transformation to international star.

Vito. "He has a way of talking to people, getting them to work with him as a team, and that's something I've always felt was an attractive reason to work with him."

Vito licensed Celine's French work, sort of a "test" before the company agreed to sign her outright. Under their agreement, CBS wouldn't own the master tracks, but they'd have the right to release them. They also contracted an option to be the first company with the right to sign her both as a French and English artist.

Then Rene made one more change: replacing Eddy Marnay, Celine's beloved songwriter. He says this was the most difficult decision he's ever made in his career because of how close they'd both become to Eddy. Still, he knew Celine needed more updated, up-tempo songs, and that wasn't Eddy's style.

"I always felt like I was Eddy's daughter . . . why would I sing other words, other writers' songs? I felt that I was cheating, and I felt that I was letting him down," says Celine. "I didn't want anyone other than him writing songs for my life. Rene said, 'Trust me, I love Eddy as much as you do,

and this is hard for me as well, but we're not letting him go. We'll still be friends, we'll still see him.'"

When Celine began recording with songwriter Luc Plamondon, she felt awkward and resentful at first, but she couldn't ignore that he was writing great material for her. Later, she knew it was the right thing to do for her career, but it wasn't until Eddy voiced his approval of her new work that she could feel comfortable again.

Incognito (1987) was Celine's first album with CBS Records (now Sony BMG), and the first the world had seen of her since her "cocoon" stage, where she'd hidden away until her butterfly wings were ready. Gone were the songs about first crushes, grandmothers, and innocence; Luc had written her an edgier album with lyrics about sexuality, romantic breakups, and secret loves. She made the transition from child star to adult siren seamlessly.

This was the year when Rene hired many of the musicians and crew who are still with Celine today, including musical director Claude "Mego" Lemay, tour director Suzanne Gingue,

ABOVE: On the day Celine signed with CBS Records (now Sony BMG) in Canada, in 1986, with (clockwise from Celine) Paul Farberman, Vito Luprano, Rene, Bill Rotari, and Don Oates. **RIGHT:** With Luc Plamondon, who wrote many of Celine's French hits.

lighting director Yves Aucoin, and sound engineer Denis Savage. Denis remembers those early years fondly. "That show we did for *Incognito* was a mix of all sorts of stuff. She used to do impersonations during the show, like she had a whole thing where she was doing Michael Jackson's 'Bad,' with choreography and a costume and everything. Mego was in a piano bar, telling the audience at the bar, 'You won't believe who was here last week—Michael Jackson!' There was a whole comedy set-up between Mego and Celine. It was really good!"

For Mego, just hooking up with Celine and Rene is a happy memory. "A guy working with Rene asked me if I was interested in playing with Celine," he recalls. "I was heavy into rock-and-roll music, so I said, 'I don't think you're calling the right guy for the job.' The guy told me to listen to the TV special she was doing that Sunday and then give them an answer. So I watched the show, and it was a new look for her, new music, and it sounded interesting to me. I said, 'That's a good change. Okay, I'll go for it.' But the first time I refused! Imagine today how I would feel!"

Suzanne never intended to enter show business. She was working as a part-time real estate agent when her friend, impersonator Jean Guy Moreau, asked her to organize his tour. Soon, director/producer Jean Bissonnette recommended Suzanne to Rene for a tour director job. Suzanne told Rene, "'I'm the kind of person who likes to stay home with my husband and my nine cats. I'm not a social person, so why did this happen to me when there are so many people who really *want* to be in this business?' Rene said, 'That's probably the reason you can do it, because you're not distracted by all the show business and meeting people.'"

Suzanne and Celine grew close over those early, exciting years. "During the holiday season, we'd go past by people's houses and see Christmas trees in the windows. We were working so late, sometimes until three or four o'clock in the morning, and we'd ask the driver to bring us to any drugstore that was open. Then we'd take a basket and buy anything that looked Christmasy. Anything red that we could do something with. Not real decorations. Then we'd go to the hotel and decorate our room . . . When room service came the next morning, everything looked so funky because we made the decorations ourselves!"

BUT JUST LIKE A BROKEN BONE CAN SIDELINE an athlete's career, an overworked voice can "break," too. And the tour for *Incognito* broke Celine's in 1988.

"The doctor gave me a shot, and I took so many vitamins, maybe steroids," she says. "I went on for the first song. The second song there was no voice coming out, and there was a guitar solo where I had to do a costume change. The guitar solo lasted about five minutes and I never came back," she says, still shuddering from the memory. "I couldn't talk. The people weren't stupid—they knew I couldn't sing. Rene went onstage and I was crying so hard in my dressing room. I heard Rene talking to them and the people started to sing a song to me. I remember hearing every seat of the house . . . you know when you stand up at a movie theater the seats go *click*? I could hear *click, click, click,* and I always think it's over. I always think the book is closed."

A doctor in Montreal told her she had polyps in her throat and would need an operation, but sent her to another doctor in New York for a second opinion. Dr. William Gould, then nearly eighty-two years old, was a renowned voice doctor with "thank you" letters on his wall from greats like Frank Sinatra, John F. Kennedy, and Walter Cronkite. Luckily, Dr. Gould opted for a less invasive but more time-consuming treatment: a complete overhaul in Celine's vocal training.

To start, she was ordered to be silent for three weeks, just in time for the Christmas holidays. Later, the doctor admitted to Rene that he didn't think she would have succeeded, but she did. When she came back in, the doctor said, "Your vocal cords are perfect." He was impressed, but wasn't ready to let her go with a simple, temporary fix. "You have a great voice, but you can't sing," he said. "You don't know how to sing, and when you start touring it's going to happen again. How serious are you about singing?"

She said, "It's my life. I want to sing all my life."

"Okay, then you have to learn how to sing."

He referred them to a doctor who was also an opera singer, William Riley, who taught her to look at every aspect of her life differently. This doctor made such a difference in her life that he is still her coach today; he comes to Las Vegas for three or four days at a time to work with her.

He showed her how to practice unusual vocal exercises that she was expected to do every day, to sneeze without making a sound, to keep herself well-hydrated on plane trips, to change her diet; her main mission in life would be to protect her fragile vocal cords.

On her days off from 1988 through 2000, she never spoke. Did it drive Rene crazy? "On the contrary," he says with a smile. They even learned to communicate with finger taps on the phone. Before the people around her got used to her periods of silence, they'd respond strangely—either they'd whisper to her or talk really loudly and slowly, using sign language as if something were wrong with her hearing. *Are these people out of their minds? I'm just having a rest!* she thought.

There was a meditative sense about these times for her, as if the world were in slow motion and all of her senses were heightened. The ocean seemed bluer, music more beautiful, and she'd appreciate the smallest details, like grains of sand under her toes and gentle wind on her arms.

Recovered physically and rested emotionally, Celine performed in the Eurovision Song Contest in Dublin, Ireland, later that year. This competition launched the careers of artists such as ABBA and Julio Iglesias. Because her songwriters were Swiss, Celine entered on behalf of Switzerland with "Ne Partez Pas Sans Moi (Don't Leave Without Me)." In front of the 600-million-person worldwide audience, Celine wowed. Rene was not surprised.

"I think she always knew she was the best, even when she was young. When she hits the stage, when she was young and today, she's sure of herself. That's the only place where she was secure. Outside the stage, she's still today insecure."

Music producer Christopher Neil was watching the show from London with his friends. They saw it as a bit of a joke and usually watched it just to make fun of the singers, whom they deemed cabaret-quality, but then someone ruined

---

RIGHT: Celine's biography from the Eurovision program in 1988, when she sang "Ne Partez Pas Sans Moi" for Switzerland.

SWITZERLAND / SUISSE

NE PARTEZ PAS SANS MOI

CELINE DION

NELLA MARTINETTI
ATILLA SEREFTUG

ATILLA SEREFTUG

CELINE DION

Celine Dion, who comes from Montreal, released her first record in 1981 at the age of 13. A year later the title song from her first L.P. won a gold medal at the Yamaha World Popular Song Festival in Tokyo. She also received the Musicians' Prize. In 1983 she received four Felix Trophies from Quebec's Recording and Entertainment Industry Association - including 'Female Performer of the Year'. In 1984, a 5-week engagement at the Paris Olympia with Patrick Sebastien was a sell-out. Celine now works in Paris and Rome where she records with some of today's leading composers. Her latest L.P. "Incognito" was released in 1987.

NELLA MARTINETTI

Nella Martinetti is one of the most prominent figures on the Swiss musical scene. She writes music and lyrics and is also a popular performer. To date she has released 10 LP's.

She has appeared in numerous TV shows in Switzerland and abroad, and in 1986 she won awards as composer, lyricist and performer of the song "Bella Musician". This is her fourth song for the Eurovision Song Contest.

ATILLA SEREFTUG

Atilla Sereftug is a professional musician who has played with the Roland Baker Orchestra in Germany and been musical director of the prominent Swiss group, Dorados. He has composed and arranged for a number of performers in Switzerland and abroad, including "Pas Pour Moi" for Daniela Simons, which took second place for Switzerland in the 1986 Eurovision Song Contest in Bergen.

CELINE DION

Celine Dion originaire de Montréal voit sortir son premier disque en 1981, à l'âge de 13 ans. Une année plus tard la chanson-titre de son premier album gagne une médaille d'or au 13e Yamaha World Popular Song Festival à Tokyo où elle remporte aussi le Prix des Musiciens. En 1983 au gala de l'Advisq (l'Association du disque et de l'industrie du spectacle québécois) elle reçoit 4 trophées Felix. En 1984 un contrat est signé à Paris pour un passage de cinq semaines à l'Olympia avec le très populaire Patrick Sébastien, cinq semaines de salles combles assurées. Depuis à Paris et à Rome, elle a enregistré des chansons par des compositeurs bien connus. Son dernier album "Incognito" est sorti l'année dernière.

NELLA MARTINETTI

Nella Martinetti est très connue dans le monde musical suisse. Elle compose musique et paroles et est aussi une interprète connue. Elle a déjà publié 10 LP.

Elle s'est produite dans de nombreux shows de télévision en Suisse et à l'étranger et en 1986 elle a gagné un prix comme compositeur-parolier et interprète de la chanson "Bella Musician". C'est la quatrième chanson qu'elle présente au Concours Eurovision de la Chanson.

ATILLA SEREFTUG

Atilla Sereftug est un musicien professionel qui a joué avec l'Orchestre Roland Baker en Allemagne et a été le chef d'orchestre de l'important groupe suisse Dorados. Il a composé et arrangé des chansons pour un grand nombre d'interprètes en Suisse et à l'étranger; l'une d'elles, "Pas Pour Moi" pour Daniela Simons a remporté la deuxième place pour la Suisse au Concours Eurovision de la Chanson 1986 à Bergen.

their insult-flinging fun. "There was a little girl singing in French for Switzerland, and we all agreed at the table that the competition is very cheesy and the song was a bit cheesy, but the girl had a fantastic voice," he said.

She won the competition.

FOR HER FIRST ENGLISH RELEASE, CBS HAD originally offered $25,000 to have Celine record the vocals to *Incognito* in English, using the musical tracks from the French album. Rene agreed to it to get her foot in the door, but three events raised the ante.

At CBS's 1987 Canadian convention, she sang a duet with Dan Hill in English that impressed CBS Canada's president Bernie DiMatteo enough to raise the budget to $100,000 so they could commission some original songs. A

few weeks later, she was asked to sing at the Juno Awards (Canada's version of the Grammys). Every year, the producers would invite Quebec's best-selling French singer to perform, but Rene didn't want her to sing in French.

"If she did that, I knew nobody would listen in English Canada, so she did a song from *Incognito* in English, and she stole the show. It was unbelievable!" he says. He spoke to Bernie DiMatteo again, and the budget rose to $300,000.

Carol Reynolds, executive producer of the Juno Awards, and a huge fan of Celine's, brought a tape of the performance to David Foster, who "freaked out." David then had a conference call with Rene to tell Bernie that $300,000 wasn't enough to compete with the superstars . . . so they received an unlimited budget. It wound up costing $600,000.

Richard Zuckerman, then vice president of A&R at CBS Records, tapped Christopher Neil to produce songs for

ABOVE: Recording *Unison* with producer David Foster in 1989.

Celine's first English album. Christopher didn't recognize her name, but as soon as he heard that she was the girl who had won the Eurovision contest, he got excited.

He came up with a few songs he thought would be appropriate, and Celine and Rene met him in a hotel restaurant in London to talk business. A pianist played in the corner while they ate, and Celine couldn't resist—every time he played a song she knew, she sang under her breath.

"I remember thinking, 'This girl is born to be onstage.' We're having a business meeting at the table, the pianist is on the other side of the room, and she *had* to sing along," Christopher says with a grin. Celine and Rene were equally impressed with him and fell in love with his songs. "She flew all the way over to London just to get the keys of the songs, then flew back. That was never going to happen again. That was the first and last time she flew to me . . . from then on, I flew to her!"

The album *Unison* was a marked change from her earlier recording sessions. Most amusing to Christopher was that Celine seemed shocked when he asked for her input; she told him that she had always been instructed before, and no one had ever asked for her opinion. After giving her some instruction, Christopher remembers telling her, "You're the artist—you've got to sing it for the rest of your life. I want it to fit comfortably on your shoulders."

The first song Celine recorded was "The Last To Know." "After she sang the first take, for the first time in my professional career, I really didn't know what to say," says Christopher. "I was desperately thinking of something reasonably intelligent to say after she finished it. In the control room, everyone was completely gobsmacked. I pressed the talkback button and said, 'Celine, that was absolutely wonderful. We'll keep that and do another one.' She said, 'Okay,' and my engineer turned to me and said . . . '*Why?*'" Celine was so nervous after each first take that she would make coffee or tea for everyone in the studio, just to have something to do while she waited for the reaction.

Christopher knew they had a potential hit record once she sang "Where Does My Heart Beat Now?," but even beyond that, he had lofty predictions for her career. On a satellite feed for a Montreal television show, he told the French-Canadian audience what he thought of their little star.

"'This girl is going to be big, and I'm not talking about big just in Canada or the UK . . . she's going to be a global star.' And they all kind of laughed, thinking I was just being polite. I mean, this is before she made it in America or anywhere else. I said, 'You don't understand what you have here . . . this is a colossal international artist.'"

Christopher wasn't the only one of her new producers who was blown away by her talent. David Foster and his wife drove a hundred miles in the rain to watch Celine sing in a tent in Montreal after he and his coworker Humberto Gatica watched the Juno videotape that Carol Reynolds sent. Seeing her perform live justified the drive.

David invited her to his place in Malibu to record tracks for *Unison*. She stood quietly in front of a microphone and waited for instructions from him. Behind Celine was a window that overlooked David's new tennis court, though, and construction had just been finished that morning.

"I said to Celine, 'I don't know if you can understand this, but we just got this tennis court, they just took the tarp down, and we just want to try bouncing the ball on it.' She said, 'Okay,' and Humberto and I got carried away and played a whole set. She could see us through the window. She stood at that microphone the entire time—she didn't move. We came back forty-five minutes later and she was still standing there. Isn't that awful?"

Not as awful as when Celine tells it. "He lies!" she says. "It was an *hour* and forty-five minutes. I was there!"

David describes his main talent as having the instinct to find singers who can truly sing, not just people who can have a hit album. He, too, saw greatness in Celine's future. "People will sometimes introduce me and say, 'He discovered Celine Dion.' Most of the time I correct them," says David. "Success has many fathers. There were many people around at the time who had a hand in her success. But in my weakest moments, sometimes I say, 'That's right. That's me!'"

The record company was thrilled with her album. But being signed with CBS Records Canada didn't mean that Celine's records would be released around the world, no

matter what language they were in. Each of CBS's territories had the right to decide which albums to release, so all the work she put into it might not have gotten her any further than the English-speaking market in Canada.

"I came back to CBS just to work with Celine as the head of international marketing," says Dave Platel, who had been working at RCA. "My job was to take her first English album and go around the world with it. I'd say, 'This is our new Canadian singer,' and through a series of presentations and cajoling and arm-twisting, I'd try to get the other territories to release that record."

Dave and his boss, Paul Burger, presented Celine's album to Tommy Mottola, president of CBS Records. He directed them to two labels: Epic (run by Dave Glew) and Columbia (run by Donnie Ienner).

"Columbia had just released Mariah Carey, so they weren't very interested in trying to break another female singer," says Rene. "Dave Glew thought that Celine was great, but everything stayed the way it was. The record was released in Canada in March, and even though we did a Canadian tour, they weren't playing the record in English Canada. The only place we sold records was in Quebec. There, we sold 125,000 records."

Everything changed in the summer of 1990. Rene was on vacation in Las Vegas with Paul Burger, who told him that the CBS Records convention that year would be in Quebec for the first time. All the heads of CBS's around the world would meet at Chateau Frontenac. Rene suggested that Celine should sing there, but Paul said, "There are no performances—it's only business. Every country has thirty minutes to talk about their upcoming products." Rene was convincing, though, so Paul made a phone call to ask if he could have someone sing. The organizers said he could do whatever he wanted with his thirty minutes.

"We knew everyone in Quebec City," says Rene, "so I said to Mario Lefebvre [Celine's Montreal CBS promotion rep at the time], we've got to get the biggest and best sound system for when Celine does her song." Mario, who is now vice president for Feeling Productions, rounded up his contacts in town and, the night before the convention opened, set up a monster P.A. system that would surely deliver Celine's voice to the thousand-plus CBS delegates. "We all knew this was our big chance, so we had to make sure everything was right," said Mario. "Celine was a very, very, big star in the francophone world, but she had to prove herself all over again in the English marketplace."

"Celine sang one song—'Where Does My Heart Beat Now?' I remember the scene as all these people stood up and went crazy, then they wanted to meet her quickly. So we met in New York and made plans to put out the record in the United States with Epic and Dave Glew, who's been her best supporter ever since that day," Rene said.

From July to September, she did showcases all over the world. Sony would organize about a hundred members of the media, and Celine would sing four or five songs live to a backing track. In the U.S., she attended dozens of record store conventions.

"That's what everybody flipped over," says Dave Platel. "Everybody who heard that massive voice coming from this diminutive singer—once they witnessed it for themselves rather than just hearing it on the CD, it connected."

The business of choosing singles is an important and inexact science. Singles are meant to be released a few weeks ahead of the albums they're on, and they can drive sales if they get good radio airplay. But it's a guessing game sometimes; the songs that are Celine's favorites or Sony Canada's favorites may not be the biggest hits, and sometimes different territories choose different singles to promote because cultural tastes don't always match.

ABOVE: Celine with the ad for *Unison* at Tower Records in Los Angeles, 1990. **LEFT:** In Quebec City with Mario Lefebvre, a longtime collaborator, c. 1987-88.

Billboard® **HOT 100 SINGLES**™

FOR WEEK ENDING MARCH 2, 1991

COMPILED FROM A NATIONAL SAMPLE OF RETAIL STORE AND ONE-STOP SALES REPORTS AND RADIO PLAYLISTS.

THIS WEEK	LAST WEEK	2 WKS AGO	WKS. ON CHART	TITLE / PRODUCER (SONGWRITER)	ARTIST / LABEL & NUMBER/DISTRIBUTING LABEL
1	1	2	11	★★ No. 1 ★★ 2 weeks at No. 1 ALL THE MAN THAT I NEED N.M.WALDEN (D.PITCHFORD,M.GORE)	◆ WHITNEY HOUSTON (C) (V) ARISTA 2156
2	4	5	7	SOMEDAY ● R.WAKE (M.CAREY,B.MARGULIES)	◆ MARIAH CAREY (C) (CD) (M) (T) (V) COLUMBIA 38-73561
3	3	3	11	ONE MORE TRY TIMMY T. (TIMMY T.)	◆ TIMMY T. (C) (T) QUALITY 15114
4	5	6	13	WHERE DOES MY HEART BEAT NOW C.NEIL (R.W.JOHNSON,T.RHODES)	◆ CELINE DION (C) EPIC 34-73536
5	2	1	16	GONNA MAKE YOU SWEAT ▲ R.CLIVILLES,D.COLE (R.CLIVILLES,F.B.WILLIAMS)	◆ C&C MUSIC FACTORY FEAT. FREEDOM WILLIAMS (C) (CD) (M) (T) COLUMBIA 38-73604
6	7	11	14	WICKED GAME E.JACOBSEN (C.ISAAK)	◆ CHRIS ISAAK (C) (V) REPRISE 4-19704
7	11	17	13	SHOW ME THE WAY D.DEYOUNG (D.DEYOUNG)	◆ STYX (C) A&M 1536
8	13	18	7	ALL THIS TIME H.PADGHAM,STING (STING)	◆ STING (C) (CD) A&M 1541
9	12	15	14	AROUND THE WAY GIRL ● M.MARL (M.WILLIAMS,J.T.SMITH,R.JAMES)	◆ L.L. COOL J (C) (CD) (M) (T) DEF JAM 38-73609/COLUMBIA
10	17	26	6	COMING OUT OF THE DARK E.ESTEFAN,JR.,J.CASAS,C.OSWALD (G.ESTEFAN,E.ESTEFAN,JR.,J.SECADA)	◆ GLORIA ESTEFAN (C) (V) EPIC 34-73666
11	6	4	18	THE FIRST TIME ● SURFACE (B.JACKSON,B.SIMPSON)	◆ SURFACE (C) (V) COLUMBIA 38-73502
12	10	12	14	I SAW RED B.HILL (J.LANE)	◆ WARRANT (C) (V) COLUMBIA 38-73597
13	15	22	11	THIS HOUSE M.SHERROD,P.SHERROD (M.SHERROD,P.SHERROD,SIR SPENCE)	◆ TRACIE SPENCER (C) (T) CAPITOL 44652
14	16	25	12	GET HERE R.ORZABAL,D.BASCOMBE (B.RUSSELL)	◆ OLETA ADAMS (C) FONTANA 878 476-4/MERCURY
15	NEW ▶		1	★★★HOT SHOT DEBUT★★★ RESCUE ME MADONNA,S.PETTIBONE (MADONNA,S.PETTIBONE)	MADONNA (C) (V) SIRE 19490/WARNER BROS.
16	19	21	17	IF YOU NEEDED SOMEBODY T.THOMAS (B.HOWE,T.THOMAS)	◆ BAD COMPANY (C) ATCO 4-98872
17	22	30	7	WAITING FOR LOVE R.NEIGHER (B.WALKER,J.PARIS)	◆ ALIAS (C) EMI 50337
18	21	27	8	IESHA D.AUSTIN (D.AUSTIN,M.BIVINS)	◆ ANOTHER BAD CREATION (C) (M) (T) MOTOWN 2070
19	25	32	7	HOLD YOU TIGHT J.SMITH,T.ROY (HAMMOND,ROY,SMITH)	◆ TARA KEMP (C) (M) (T) GIANT 4-19458
20	24	31	9	SIGNS D.MCCLENDON (L.EMMERSON)	◆ TESLA (C) GEFFEN 4-19653
21	23	28	12	DEEPER SHADE OF SOUL J.M.A.,URBAN DANCE SQUAD (U.D.S.,R.BARRETTO)	◆ URBAN DANCE SQUAD (C) (T) (V) ARISTA 2026
22	14	13	14	LOVE MAKES THINGS HAPPEN L.A.REID,BABYFACE (BABYFACE,L.A.REID)	◆ PEBBLES (C) MCA 53973
23	8	7	14	I'LL GIVE ALL MY LOVE TO YOU K.SWEAT (K.SWEAT,B.WOOTEN)	◆ KEITH SWEAT (C) VINTERTAINMENT 4-64915/ELEKTRA
24	27	33	13	ROUND AND ROUND PRINCE (PRINCE)	◆ TEVIN CAMPBELL (C) (CD) (M) (T) (V) PAISLEY PARK 4-19748/WARNER BROS.
25	32	38	4	I'VE BEEN THINKING ABOUT YOU M.PHILLIPS (HENSHALL,HELMS,CHANDLER,CHAMBERS)	◆ LONDONBEAT (M) (T) RADIOACTIVE 53992*/MCA
26	9	8	15	DISAPPEAR C.THOMAS (J.FARRISS,M.HUTCHENCE)	◆ INXS (C) (V) ATLANTIC 4-87784
27	31	35	7	WAITING FOR THAT DAY G.MICHAEL (G.MICHAEL,M.JAGGER,K.RICHARDS)	GEORGE MICHAEL (C) (V) COLUMBIA 38-73663
28	34	36	8	I'LL DO 4 U M.ROONEY,M.MORALES (D.PAICH,C.LYNN,D.FOSTER,FATHER M.C.)	◆ FATHER M.C. (C) (M) (T) UPTOWN 53914/MCA
29	36	44	4	YOU'RE IN LOVE G.BALLARD (WILSON PHILLIPS,G.BALLARD)	◆ WILSON PHILLIPS (C) (CD) SBK 07346
30	20	10	16	LOVE WILL NEVER DO (WITHOUT YOU) ● J.JAM,T.LEWIS (J.HARRIS III,T.LEWIS)	◆ JANET JACKSON (C) (T) (V) A&M 1538
31	37	45	5	I'LL BE BY YOUR SIDE STEVIE B (STEVIE B,D.ATABAY)	STEVIE B (C) LMR 2758/RCA
32	18	9	13	PLAY THAT FUNKY MUSIC ● EARTHQUAKE (VANILLA ICE,R.PARISSI)	◆ VANILLA ICE (C) (M) (T) SBK 07339
33	29	20	24	HIGH ENOUGH ● R.NEVISON (TOMMY,JACK,TED)	◆ DAMN YANKEES (C) (V) WARNER BROS. 4-19595
34	41	59	5	★★★POWER PICK/SALES★★★ RICO SUAVE M.SEMBELLO (GERARDO,C.WARREN)	◆ GERARDO (C) (T) INTERSCOPE 4-98871/EAST WEST
35	43	65	4	SADENESS PART 1 ENIGMA (CURLY M.C.,F.GREGORIAN,D.FAIRSTEIN)	◆ ENIGMA (C) (M) (T) CHARISMA 4-98864
36	28	16	18	AFTER THE RAIN M.TANNER,D.THOENER (M.NELSON,G.NELSON,M.TANNER,R.WILSON)	◆ NELSON (C) (V) DGC 4-19667
37	26	14	18	SENSITIVITY ● J.JAM,T.LEWIS (J.HARRIS III,T.LEWIS)	◆ RALPH TRESVANT (C) (CD) (M) (T) (V) MCA 53932
38	46	50	8	SOMETHING IN MY HEART DR.DRE (MICHEL'LE,L.A.DRE,DR.DRE)	◆ MICHEL'LE (C) RUTHLESS 4-98885/ATCO
39	49	77	3	MERCY MERCY ME (THE ECOLOGY)/I WANT YOU T.MACERO (M.GAYE,A.ROSS,L.WARE)	ROBERT PALMER (C) EMI 50344
40	45	52	5	MY SIDE OF THE BED D.KAHNE (S.HOFFS,T.KELLY,B.STEINBERG)	◆ SUSANNA HOFFS (C) COLUMBIA 38-73529
41	30	23	13	MONEYTALKS B.FAIRBAIRN (A.YOUNG,M.YOUNG)	◆ AC/DC (C) (V) ATCO 4-98881
42	47	51	6	CHASIN' THE WIND R.NEVISON (D.WARREN)	◆ CHICAGO (C) (V) REPRISE 4-19466
43	33	19	27	HEAT OF THE MOMENT L.A.REID,BABYFACE (L.A.REID,BABYFACE)	◆ AFTER 7 (C) (M) (T) VIRGIN 4-96553
44	59	86	3	CRY FOR HELP G.STEVENSON,R.ASTLEY (R.ASTLEY,R.FISHER)	◆ RICK ASTLEY (C) (V) RCA 2774
45	35	34	11	IT NEVER RAINS (IN SOUTHERN CALIFORNIA) TONY!TONI!TONE! (R.WIGGINS,T.CHRISTIAN)	◆ TONY! TONI! TONE! (C) (T) (V) WING 879 068-4/MERCURY
46	48	53	5	MOTHER'S PRIDE G.MICHAEL (G.MICHAEL)	GEORGE MICHAEL (C) (V) COLUMBIA 38-73663
47	38	24	19	JUST ANOTHER DREAM DANCIN' DANNY D,S.PETTIBONE (C.DENNIS,D.POKU)	◆ CATHY DENNIS (C) (CD) (M) (T) (V) POLYDOR 877 962-4/PLG
48	75	—	2	★★★POWER PICK/AIRPLAY★★★ BABY BABY K.THOMAS (A.GRANT,K.THOMAS)	◆ AMY GRANT (C) A&M 1549
49	53	68	4	JUST THE WAY IT IS, BABY THE REMBRANDTS (SOLEM,WILDE)	◆ THE REMBRANDTS (C) ATCO 4-98874
50	40	37	22	FROM A DISTANCE ▲ A.MARDIN (J.GOLD)	◆ BETTE MIDLER (C) (V) ATLANTIC 4-87820
51	52	61	5	RIDE THE WIND B.FAIRBAIRN (B.DALL,C.C.DEVILLE,B.MICHAELS,R.ROCKETT)	◆ POISON (C) ENIGMA 44616/CAPITOL
52	39	29	16	I'M NOT IN LOVE B.ROSENBERG (G.GOULDMAN,E.STEWART)	WILL TO POWER (C) (V) EPIC 34-73636
53	57	69	5	TOGETHER FOREVER C.BERRIOS (C.BERRIOS,F.REYES,F.KALAVE)	LISETTE MELENDEZ (C) (M) (T) FEVER 38-73630/COLUMBIA
54	63	85	3	HOW TO DANCE M.NEUMAYER (K.BIEDERMANN,P.PFAB,H.WOLFGRUBER)	◆ BINGO BOYS (C) (M) (T) ATLANTIC 4-87756
55	54	57	7	SURE LOOKIN' D.GAMSON (D.OSMOND,D.GAMSON,LEMANS)	◆ DONNY OSMOND (C) (T) CAPITOL 44670
56	58	75	4	EASY COME EASY GO B.HILL (K.WINGER)	◆ WINGER (C) ATLANTIC 4-87773
57	NEW ▶		1	JOYRIDE C.OFWERMAN (P.GESSLE)	◆ ROXETTE (C) EMI 50342
58	50	39	11	SPEND MY LIFE D.STRUM,M.SLAUGHTER (D.STRUM,M.SLAUGHTER)	◆ SLAUGHTER (C) CHRYSALIS 23605
59	66	83	4	FUNK BOUTIQUE T.MORAN,A.PANDA (T.MORAN,A.TRIPOLI)	THE COVER GIRLS (C) (M) (T) EPIC 34-73698
60	83	—	2	CALL IT POISON P.WOLF (THE ESCAPE CLUB)	◆ THE ESCAPE CLUB (C) (T) ATLANTIC 4-87759
61	42	46	9	I'VE BEEN WAITING FOR YOU S.CUTLER (S.CUTLER,A.ARMATO)	◆ GUYS NEXT DOOR (C) SBK 07340
62	51	47	9	POWER OF LOVE DEEE-LITE (DEEE-LITE)	◆ DEEE-LITE (C) (CD) (M) (T) (V) ELEKTRA 4-64912
63	62	67	6	NIGHT AND DAY A.MARDIN (R.SEEMAN,B.HUGHES)	BETTE MIDLER (C) (V) ATLANTIC 4-87825
64	67	74	5	SECRET R.ZITO (F.GOLDE,B.ROBERTS)	◆ HEART (C) CAPITOL 44614
65	55	48	11	THIS IS PONDEROUS M.NEALY,J.BLANEY (J.BLANEY,M.NEALY,P.DE VAULT,T.MARTIN)	2NU (C) (V) ATLANTIC 4-87771
66	61	60	9	HERE COMES THE HAMMER M.C.HAMMER (M.C.HAMMER)	◆ M.C. HAMMER (C) (T) CAPITOL 44572
67	44	41	9	DON'T HOLD BACK YOUR LOVE D.TYSON (R.PAGE,G.O'BRIEN,D.TYSON)	◆ DARYL HALL JOHN OATES (C) (V) ARISTA 2157
68	84	96	3	TEMPLE OF LOVE D.BRIDGEMAN (FRANGLEN,ROBERTS)	◆ HARRIET (C) (T) EAST WEST 4-98863
69	85	—	2	STONE COLD GENTLEMAN D.SIMMONS,KAYO (D.SIMMONS,KAYO,L.A.REID,L.JOHNSON)	◆ RALPH TRESVANT (C) MCA 54043
70	56	42	13	I DON'T KNOW ANYBODY ELSE GROOVE GROOVE MELODY (M.LIMONI,D.DAVOLI,V.SEMPLICI)	◆ BLACK BOX (C) (CD) (T) RCA 2751
71	81	—	2	LET'S CHILL T.RILEY (T.RILEY,B.BELLE)	◆ GUY (M) (T) UPTOWN 54051*/MCA
72	80	93	3	ANOTHER SLEEPLESS NIGHT M.WILSON (M.WILSON,T.AMOS)	SHAWN CHRISTOPHER (C) (T) ARISTA 2148
73	90	—	2	I LIKE THE WAY (THE KISSING GAME) T.RILEY (T.RILEY,B.BELL,D.WAY)	◆ HI-FIVE (C) (M) (T) JIVE 1424/RCA
74	60	54	21	MILES AWAY B.HILL (P.TAYLOR)	◆ WINGER (C) ATLANTIC 4-87824
75	74	82	22	UNCHAINED MELODY ▲ B.MEDLEY (H.ZARET,A.NORTH)	THE RIGHTEOUS BROTHERS (C) CURB 76842
76	94	—	2	I LOVE YOU K.SHARP (VANILLA ICE,K.SHARP)	◆ VANILLA ICE (C) (T) SBK 07346
77	70	64	15	THE SHOOP SHOOP SONG (IT'S IN HIS KISS) P.ASHER (R.CLARK)	◆ CHER (C) (V) GEFFEN 4-19659
78	NEW ▶		1	TOUCH ME (ALL NIGHT LONG) C.DENNIS,P.BODGER,S.PETTIBONE (C.DENNIS,C.DELYLE GREGORY,P.ADAMS)	◆ CATHY DENNIS (C) (M) (T) POLYDOR 879 466-4/PLG
79	71	62	14	NO MATTER WHAT M.LIGGETT,C.BARBOSA (A.GODWIN,L.LANGE)	◆ GEORGE LAMOND (DUET WITH BRENDA K. STARR) (C) COLUMBIA 38-73603
80	73	63	7	WHEN WILL I SEE YOU SMILE AGAIN? T.GATLING,A.STEWART (T.GATLING,A.STEWART)	◆ BELL BIV DEVOE (C) (T) MCA 53976
81	89	—	2	ALL TRUE MAN J.JAM,T.LEWIS (T.LEWIS,J.HARRIS III)	◆ ALEXANDER O'NEAL (C) TABU 35-73627/EPIC
82	NEW ▶		1	HERE WE GO R.CLIVILLES,D.COLE (R.CLIVILLES,F.B.WILLIAMS)	C&C MUSIC FACTORY/FREEDOM WILLIAMS/ZELMA DAVIS (C) (M) (T) (V) COLUMBIA 38-73690
83	65	49	22	BECAUSE I LOVE YOU (THE POSTMAN SONG) ● STEVIE B (W.BROOKS)	◆ STEVIE B (C) (V) LMR 2724/RCA
84	69	58	25	LOVE TAKES TIME ● W.AFANASIEFF (M.CAREY,B.MARGULIES)	◆ MARIAH CAREY (C) (V) COLUMBIA 38-73455
85	72	55	25	THE WAY YOU DO THE THINGS YOU DO ● UB40 (ROBINSON,ROGERS)	◆ UB40 (C) VIRGIN 4-98978
86	68	40	16	JUSTIFY MY LOVE L.KRAVITZ (L.KRAVITZ,MADONNA)	◆ MADONNA (C) (CD) (M) (T) (V) SIRE 4-19485/WARNER BROS.
87	76	56	13	SHELTER ME J.JANSEN,T.KEIFER (J.JANSEN,T.KEIFER)	◆ CINDERELLA (C) (V) MERCURY 878 700-4
88	79	88	4	GIVE IT UP B.HAM (GIBBONS,HILL,BEARD)	◆ ZZ TOP (C) WARNER BROS. 4-19470
89	NEW ▶		1	IN YOUR ARMS B.ROCK (YOUNG,SUTTON)	LITTLE CAESAR (C) DGC 19003
90	64	43	15	CANDY D.WAS (I.POP)	◆ IGGY POP WITH KATE PIERSON (C) VIRGIN 4-98900
91	91	90	4	WHAT'S IT GONNA BE JELLYBEAN (A.PREVEN,W.POTTS)	◆ JELLYBEAN FEATURING NIKI HARIS (C) (CD) (M) (T) ATLANTIC 4-87782
92	86	78	22	WIGGLE IT ● G.MOREL (G.MOREL,R.VARGAS)	◆ 2 IN A ROOM (C) (M) (T) CUTTING 4-98887/CHARISMA
93	98	94	14	HOUSE FULL OF REASONS D.TYSON (J.COLE)	JUDE COLE (C) REPRISE 4-19530
94	78	70	18	FOR YOU J.SPINKS (J.SPINKS)	◆ THE OUTFIELD (C) (V) MCA 53935
95	82	73	5	WHO SAID I WOULD P.COLLINS,R.COLBY (P.COLLINS)	◆ PHIL COLLINS (C) ATLANTIC 4-87754
96	NEW ▶		1	THAT'S WHY S.BRAY (S.BRAY,L.MALLAH,A.FIELDS)	◆ THE PARTY (C) HOLLYWOOD 4-64903/ELEKTRA
97	77	72	9	REMEMBER MY NAME A.JOHNS,HOUSE OF LORDS (N.GRAHAM,B.MITCHELL)	◆ HOUSE OF LORDS (C) SIMMONS 2736/RCA
98	NEW ▶		1	MADE UP MY MIND M.LIGGETT,C.BARBOSA (E.GOLD)	◆ SAFIRE (C) (M) (T) MERCURY 878 784-4
99	97	97	3	STILL GOT THE BLUES G.MOORE,I.TAYLOR (G.MOORE)	◆ GARY MOORE (C) CHARISMA 4-98854
100	93	99	3	HOW CAN YOU EXPECT TO BE TAKEN SERIOUSLY? PET SHOP BOYS,H.FALTERMEYER (N.TENNANT,C.LOWE)	◆ PET SHOP BOYS (C) EMI 50343

◯ Records with the greatest airplay and sales gains this week. ◆ Videoclip availability. ● Recording Industry Assn. Of America (RIAA) certification for sales of 500,000 units. ▲ RIAA certification for sales of 1 million units, with additional million indicated by a numeral following the symbol. Catalog number is for cassette single. *Asterisk indicates catalog number is for cassette maxi-single; regular cassette single unavailable. (C) Cassette single availability. (CD) Compact disc single availability. (M) Cassette maxi-single availability. (T) 12-inch vinyl single availability. (V) 7-inch vinyl single availability. © 1991, Billboard/BPI Communications, Inc.

84 BILLBOARD MARCH 2, 1991

ABOVE: The Top 100 Singles chart for March 2, 1991, when "Where Does My Heart Beat Now" reached Number Four. **RIGHT:** Celine accepts an award for Artist of the Year at the Juno Awards in 1991, the same award show that helped launch her first album in English.

CBS chose to lead off *Unison* with "Where Does My Heart Beat Now?," a song that earned its keep quickly, reaching Number Four on the Top 100 charts in February 1991. "(If There Was) Any Other Way" hit the Top 40 soon after. The album sold more than a million copies worldwide, and earned her two Juno awards: Album of the Year and Female Vocalist of the Year.

Celine was excited . . . and scared. Her newfound overseas fame meant that she would have to do interviews and publicity appearances in English, a language she was not yet wholly comfortable with. Slang was a particular problem, and she couldn't find expressions like "yo mama" in the dictionary. Really, she thought of *Unison* as an icebreaker and thought it would take her a while to gain recognition outside of Canada.

Instead, in September 1990, she made her first appearance on *The Tonight Show*. Although it was still Johnny Carson's show, Jay Leno was to guest host that day and invited her to perform before her album ever hit the charts. And when she arrived, producers scheduled her *second* appearance before she had even performed her first.

It was a major turning point in her career, Rene says. Only after she had appeared on *The Tonight Show* did English-speaking Canada start playing her records on the radio. And when they went back to the show a few months later to launch her first single, Johnny Carson was hosting at the end of his legendary career. "When we played, we had no monitors when we started," says Mego, Celine's musical director. "I was alone on piano, and I couldn't hear myself. The sound came about fifteen seconds after. That was scary!"

ESPECIALLY ON HER EARLIEST TELEVISION interviews, Celine was focused on getting her words right and her message out, so the public didn't get to see much of her funny side. But when you ask those close with her, that's one of the first things they all comment on: her "zaniness." She has a quick, sometimes sarcastic wit, and she often throws jabs Rene's way. She's been known to dress up as the Easter Bunny and hand out baskets to her crew, or wear cow slippers that a fan gave her onstage. Right before Christmas 2004, she showed up on stage with curlers in her hair for the sound check. Just as the music started, she pressed a button and Christmas lights twinkled and blinked all over her curlers.

When the mood strikes, she has all the electric energy of Robin Williams, hopping around backstage like a Mexican jumping bean. She likes to be in the middle of the action, to be "one of the guys," and she'll gladly go along with others' schemes. With no self-consciousness about her appearance, she'll make contorted faces and dress ridiculously just to make people laugh.

If she went to a Halloween party, she wouldn't be the pretty kitty or the belly dancer. She'd come as the vagabond with a missing tooth and two black eyes, with toilet paper stuck to her shoe.

"If I tell her, 'Get in the trunk of the car,' she'll get in the trunk of the car," Dave Platel says.

While shooting the video for "I'm Alive," she finally convinced director Scott Floyd Lochmus to cut his trademark long, thick hair. As the hairdresser snipped and snipped, the hair blew out of the trailer like tumbleweeds. Celine, in her cotton tank top and skirt, gathered the hair and stuck one clump under each armpit and dangled some out of the top of her shirt. Then she ran after the tour van coming through the Universal Studios lot, waving and singing while they snapped pictures in laughing disbelief.

———

BUT THERE'S ANOTHER SIDE TO CELINE, TOO—A quiet, introspective side. After a show, the great helium balloon deflates. She sits with two porcelain cups: one with

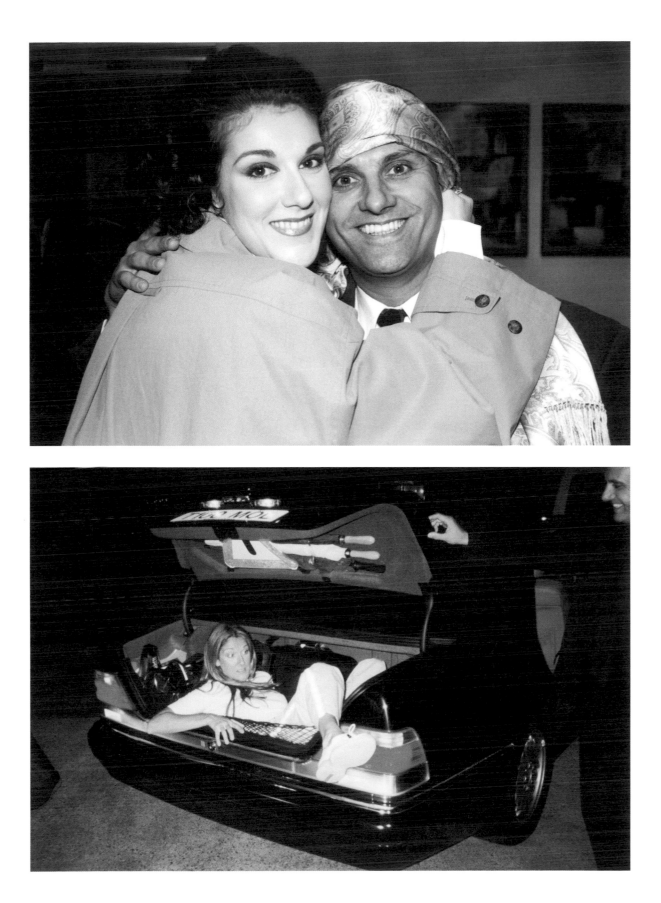

TOP: With Dave Platel, her long-time management associate, friend, and co-conspirator in goofy acts.
BOTTOM: At Dave's suggestion, Celine hopped into the trunk of a car at a private airport outside London when she arrived from Edinburgh for her shows at Wembley Stadium, July 10 and 11, 1999.

tea, one with honey, spooning the honey in generously. As the adrenaline wears out, she lets go and prefers to stop being the center of attention.

As time went on, it became harder and harder for Celine to be anything but the center of attention. Disney tapped her to sing the title song for *Beauty and the Beast* with Peabo Bryson in 1991, and her ability to "blend in" in a crowd disappeared.

Producer Walter Afanasieff met her for the first time when recording this song, and he remembers, "She

was a very interesting, unpretentious, honest, endearing, very dedicated, professional, aspiring young artist with one of the most beautiful voices I've ever heard. It was lovely working with her, and especially pairing her up with another one of my favorite voices."

Celine almost didn't agree to record the song, though. She was coming off a heartbreaking disappointment and was hardly in the mood to put herself at risk for another. After James Horner's agents saw Celine perform at the Juno Awards in Canada, they asked to meet her, and thought she'd

ABOVE: Performing with Peabo Bryson at the Capitole Theatre in Quebec City, at the recording of her first Disney special. RIGHT: A letter from Alan Menken, one of the "Beauty And The Beast" songwriters, along with Celine's pass from performing the song at the Academy Awards in 1992.

ALAN MENKEN

64th Annual
ACADEMY
AWARDS

No:
0499

CÉLINE
DION
BACKSTAGE

December 20, 1991

Ms. Celine Dion
Feeling Productions, Inc.
4 Place Laval
Suite # 500
Laval, Quebec
Canada H7N 5Y3

Dear Celine,

I must apologize for not contacting you sooner, but my work schedule has kept me distracted and constantly on the move ever since the opening of Beauty. As soon as Chris Montan suggested you as one of the vocalists on the duet version of 'Beauty And The Beast', I picked up your latest album and instantly became a fan. Your vocal on our song thrills me and watching you perform (in the video and on Good Morning America) has doubled my admiration. Together with Peabo, you have created a new highpoint in my career.

I wish you much continued success in the years to come and hope our paths cross again professionally.

Sincerely,

Alan Menken

AM:rk

19 LILY POND LANE
KATONAH, NY 10536
(914) 232-0973
FAX (914) 232-9074

MANAGEMENT:
THE SHUKAT COMPANY
340 WEST 55 STREET, SUITE 2A
NEW YORK, NY 10019

be great for the theme song for Steven Spielberg's upcoming movie, *An American Tail 2: Fievel Goes West*. Although Linda Ronstadt had great success with "Somewhere Out There," the theme from the original movie, she had turned down the opportunity to sing on the sequel's soundtrack. Celine was electric with excitement—she was going to sing in a Steven Spielberg movie! And best of all, she absolutely loved the song "Dreams To Dream," which reminded her of something her mother had written. But when Linda Ronstadt heard Celine's recording, she decided she wanted to sing the song after all, and Spielberg agreed. After all, Celine was pretty much an unknown, and Linda had already made the first soundtrack a success. James Horner lobbied hard for Celine, but it didn't change anything.

Rene was devastated. Paul Farberman, then vice president of business affairs at Universal Pictures, says, "In all the years I've known him, I've never seen him so upset. Rene was in tears. He didn't know how to tell Celine." So he waited until he had some good news for her first: She'd been chosen to sing the theme song for *Beauty and the Beast*. It was little consolation for her; she was devastated and it took some convincing before she'd do the song that wound up becoming a major milestone in her career.

The effort earned a Grammy for best pop performance by a duo, and on Celine's twenty-fourth birthday, she and Peabo sang at the Academy Awards, where the song won again. Not only did this boost her fame in the United States, it also helped to earn Celine a $10 million contract with Sony Music International for five albums, the highest sum they had ever paid a Canadian artist.

"I'm getting recognized in the streets!" Celine told an interviewer after the Oscars, with an obvious excitement in her voice. People didn't often remember her name, but they would come up to her and say, "Hey, you're that singer from 'Beauty and the Beast.'" The fact that they were paying attention to her at all was more important to her than whether or not people remembered her name. "It will come with time," she said. "We have to be patient."

Not extraordinarily patient, mind you. Her self-titled album was soon to follow, and it fanned the flames of her initial English success with hits like "If You Asked Me To," "Nothing Broken But My Heart," and "Love Can Move Mountains."

Walter Afanasieff was honored to produce for Celine again, having by now become a friend of hers, as well as Rene's. Prince, an artist Celine greatly admired, wrote "With This Tear" just for her after admiring her voice on "Beauty and the Beast." Walter remembers the cold day they recorded it in Canada fondly.

"Celine is a goofball," he says. "She'll laugh the hardest at the dirtiest jokes, have a food fight when there's a food fight that needs to be had . . . she's constantly having fun, and she's never, ever in a bad mood."

Following her lead, the staff tends to joke around and be in a good mood, too. That day, they were playing ping-pong and cracking each other up before the recording. But "With This Tear" is a song about crying and pain and loss; it couldn't come off sounding like Celine had just been laughing it up with her buddies.

"She started the song and it just wasn't working . . . she sounded happy!" Walter says. "I needed to get her to sing in the saddest voice that she could muster up. I just wanted her to be in tears, so I kept trying to explain to her, 'You have to sound a little sadder. You have to be a little more believable.' Finally I thought, *I have to do something. This girl is having too good a time!* So I took her aside and I said, 'What's the worst possible thing that you can imagine happening to you in your life right now?'"

Celine thought for a long moment and said, "My mother dying."

Walter asked her to think about that, then to take that feeling with her and use it in the song. "She went to the microphone in this very depressed state, which I obviously doused her with from the thought of losing her mother, but with that I got an incredibly sad, endearing, very beautiful vocal."

The album came out in March 1992, the year that also marked her first American tour. The next year was marked by the taping of her first television special for Disney in September. After the special aired, Rene was in his office in Montreal when the phone rang.

RIGHT: The 1993 Grammy award for her duet with Peabo Bryson on "Beauty And The Beast."

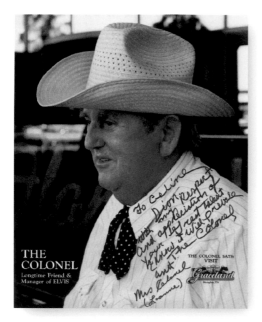

"My assistant said, 'Colonel Parker is on the phone for you.' I said, 'What?!'" The Colonel had seen Celine sing "Can't Help Falling In Love" on the television special, and her talent dazzled him. He'd called to make an offer to have Celine perform at the Las Vegas Hilton. Rene explained that he had already promised Caesars that if she ever performed in Vegas, she'd go there first. The Colonel understood, but told Rene that if he ever came to Vegas, he'd love to meet and see if they could do anything else together.

About a month later, Rene—along with the same two friends who'd gone to the Elvis tribute concert—visited The Colonel and his wife at their home. "He sat on the sofa and said, 'Rene, I rarely see someone with that type of voice and that talent. She's going to be as big as Barbra Streisand.' I wagged my finger at him and said, 'Oh, Colonel. Somebody told me once that you can never compare an artist with another artist. She'll never be Barbra Streisand. You know who told me that?'"

The Colonel didn't say a word, but just looked at Rene strangely. "I said, 'You did!' So now his eyes are stunned. I said, 'Remember you produced a show with Wayne Newton six years ago? We were there . . . ' He looked at Ben and said, 'Oh! You're the one who hustled me for pictures!' He started laughing, and I said, 'By the way, I took that great piece of advice.' We laughed about it and became very close before he passed away."

BUT EVEN WITH HER SUCCESS IN AMERICA, Celine was still finding her way in other foreign markets. "Not every market was a slam-dunk because we were competing with a lot of different artists," says Dave Platel. "We were having trouble in the U.K. for some reason—we just couldn't cross over the threshold there. So we had a show booked at the Olympia Theatre in Paris, and we decided, let's take the band over to the U.K. and do a show there . . . not Celine with a microphone and a tape in the background, but with the whole band."

They booked into a very small theatre called the Dominion Theatre and asked all of the record company staff to come out and bring their radio and press contacts. "That was probably the turning point in the U.K. for us, because they saw Celine live onstage, and you know what she's like live—she gives everything."

This was just before the album *The Colour of My Love* was released, which gave Celine a breakthrough hit in Europe with the song "Think Twice." The song was never huge in America, but it went to Number One in the U.K. and stayed there for seven weeks. The song was written by British writers, so Celine's team surmises that there was a groundswell of support for it because of its local talent. Dave

---

ABOVE: The Colonel sent this note and signed photograph to Celine and Rene as a thank you for some birthday flowers. **PREVIOUS:** In the studio with her recording team: John Doelp of Epic Records, her longtime sound engineer Humberto Gatica, and Vito Luprano, c. 1994.

says that's the song that broke Celine in to the rest of the world outside of Canada and the United States.

"When you break the U.K., it's pretty much the bellwether for the rest of the marketplace," he says. "The two strongest English-speaking markets in Europe are the U.K. and Germany. So if you can have a hit in either England or Germany, you have a really good chance of influencing the rest of the European continent and hitting the Pan-European chart."

Next, in 1995, Celine released the album *D'eux* (known in English as *The French Album*) with producer/songwriter Jean-Jacques Goldman. "Jean-Jacques is a very big star in France as a singer, and he is on the same record label, and

he's the one who went to the label and said he thought that Celine was amazing," says Rene.

Jean-Jacques says he was excited about Celine's voice because the female vocalists popular in French at the time were mostly "old-fashioned," and Celine had the best quality voice he'd heard in a long time. He asked Sony if they'd be interested in having him write more modern songs for Celine, and they certainly were. Before he began writing, he collected everything he could find that was ever written about her, including magazines, newspapers, and books. Not only does a singer need to have beautiful music and a great voice to succeed, he says, but she needs to have credibility. Listeners must believe

ABOVE: The Olympia Theatre in Paris, where Celine performed in 1994. Marc Dupre, the artist impersonator who opened for her, later married Rene's daughter, Anne-Marie, in 2000.

LETTER FROM COLONEL PARKER, FEBRUARY 23, 1994

When Celine was off on her first hiatus from show business, learning English and updating her look, Rene and several friends chanced upon a meeting with Colonel Parker, Elvis's renowned manager, in Las Vegas. At the time, Parker advised Rene never to compare his singer to anyone else—it would only be a discredit to Celine. About six years later, the Colonel happened to catch a Celine special on the Disney Channel and invited Rene to his home to talk about future plans for a potential Celine performance at the Hilton Las Vegas.

The Colonel and Rene became close friends until the Colonel passed away in 1997. The song he mentions in the letter never came to pass.

HAPPY BIRTHDAY CELINE FLYER, MARCH 30, 1996

As Celine toured more and more, the people in the band, the people arranging the tour, and the other folks she traveled with became a second family to her—and she to them. So, when the opportunity came in Brisbane to surprise her by having the audience serenade her for a change, the tour managers seized the opportunity. Just as instructed, after the second song, the lights went on, the audience rose to their feet, and together with the orchestra they serenaded Celine, who was floored.

Colonel Thomas A. Parker

POST OFFICE BOX 93118-77
LAS VEGAS, NEVADA 89193-3118

February 23, 1994

Mr. René Angélil
Mr. Ben Kaye
FEELING Productions Inc.
4 Place Laval   #500
Laval, Quebec
Canada H7N 5Y3

Good Day Rene & Ben:

I enjoyed meeting with you at the house...so did Loanne.
It was a great pleasure. I learned from you, and perhaps you
learned a little from me.

I appreciate you relaying my congratulations to Celine Dion
on her new record and her wonderful performance on the Disney channel
February 6, which I told you about while you were here.

I was amazed that in the Sunday paper there was no mention
of Celine Dion being at the concert. I had a friend and his family
visit for the weekend, and they were invited to the show, as he is
a producer and they were very impressed with Celine Dion.

As we discussed, it would be appreciated if you would send
one of her albums to Barron Hilton and Gary Greg at their addresses
below: Mr. Barron Hilton
               Chairman & Chief Executive Officer
               Hilton Hotels Corporation
               9336 Civic Center Drive
               Beverly Hills, CA 90210-3189
               U.S.A.

               Mr. Gary Gregg
               President
               Las Vegas Hilton
               3000 Paradise Rd.
               Las Vegas, Nv. 89109
               U.S.A.
Perhaps include with the album a note saying: "As requested by
our good friend, The Colonel." The rest of them you can send to us
at: Colonel Tom Parker
     953 East Sahara Ave. Suite 9-B
     Las Vegas, Nv. 89104-3012
or you can send them to the PO box address shown above.

(Continued)

the power of the dream

ABOVE: With Jean-Jacques Goldman at the press conference for *D'eux* in 1995. RIGHT: With Jean-Jacques recording "S'il Suffisait D'aimer" at Studio Mega in Paris, March 1998.

she means what she's singing, so he wanted to make sure his lyrics rang true with her experiences and personality.

Celine and Rene met with him and clicked right away. He proposed sixteen songs, all of which they loved, and the album *D'eux* emerged. In French, *d'eux* means "from them." The title was meant to signify that the album came from the two of them: Celine and Jean-Jacques. "Deux," without the apostrophe, means "two," which also worked. Within only seven months, it became the best-selling French-language album in history. It remained at the number-one spot in France for forty-four weeks, only to be replaced by Celine's next album. It has now sold 7 million copies, beating the second-best-selling French album by a whopping 3 million sales. *D'eux* also made history by being the first French album to earn a gold record in England, where it sold 250,000 copies.

This album, which Rene says is stunning because it's "smoother and softer" than most of her other work, contains many of the team's favorite songs. When asked if he has a favorite song of Celine's, without hesitating, Rene says it's "Pour Que Tu M'aimes Encore (For You To Love Me Still)," which he calls the "ultimate love song," elucidating just what a person would do for the one she loves.

Celine wasn't through building global appeal, however. After working closely with Epic/Sony in Japan for several years, they finally came up with a great idea: Soap operas are huge in Japan, so why not have Celine sing a theme song for one of their popular soaps? And with that came the single "To Love You More," written by David Foster and the multi-millionaire and former Universal Music CEO Edgar Bronfman Jr., who wrote under the pseudonym Junior Miles. *The Colour of My Love* was reedited in Japan to add the track to the album. "We sold over a million records in Japan based on the strength of that one song," says Dave Platel.

But it would be her next album, *Falling Into You* (1996), that would become the overall fan favorite in English. This

album seemed to push the boundaries of Celine's voice to bring out an unparalleled power and maturity. She worked with a mix of familiar producers and new-to-her producers, such as Jim Steinman, best known for working with Meatloaf, who wrote and produced her smash hit "It's All Coming Back To Me Now"; and Ric Knowles and Billy Steinberg, who wrote and produced the title track "Falling Into You." The single "All By Myself" shows an anguished, raw side of Celine rarely heard in her generally cheerful pop songs.

"The big note at the end, where I put the key change, is so hard to do it's almost inhuman," says David Foster. "She did it the first time and it was numbing. Everybody in the control room just went, 'Oh my God,' and me being the jerk that I am, I said, 'That was really good. Let's try a couple more.' She looked at me like, *Do you have any idea how hard that was even for me?* To her credit, she tried a couple more times. I burned her throat right out, and we ended up using the first take because it was perfect."

The album's magnificence is marked by one controversy: The legendary producer Phil Spector came out of semi-retirement to work with Celine, but ended up clashing with her team and the collaboration fell apart. Though he praised Celine's talent, he walked out in a huff and never gave Sony the recordings.

"The only thing I can tell you is that it's too bad what happened because there were two songs in there that were like jewels, and unfortunately we'll never hear them," Rene says. But the missing Spector songs didn't stop the album from selling 29 million copies.

That July, Celine was selected to perform "The Power Of The Dream" at the opening ceremonies of the Summer Olympics in Atlanta. The Olympic committee wanted an American to sing the song, but Bill Clinton agreed that Celine should perform. It remains one of her most thrilling memories, not only because it was such an exciting performance, but also because of a special surprise set up for her.

Gymnast Nadia Comaneci, the first person ever to score a perfect 10 in the Olympics, was the only person who almost derailed Celine's career path. Celine remembers watching Nadia's perfect routine on television when she was

---

ABOVE: With Nadia Comaneci and the special "Perfect 10" watch Nadia gave her. **TOP LEFT:** With President Bill Clinton at the 1996 Atlanta Olympics. **BOTTOM LEFT:** With the young dancers at the Atlanta Olympics.

about eight years old and says she was so impressed that she wanted to be just like Nadia. Celine's team knew this, so they asked Nadia to visit Celine's dressing room.

"I told her she was my idol and I was crying," says Celine. "She gave me a watch with the perfect score on the back. It was an incredible thrill."

Less than a year later came the *Let's Talk About Love* album, full of collaborations with artists like Carole King, The Bee Gees, Barbra Streisand, and Luciano Pavarotti. Due to scheduling conflicts, Barbra and Celine weren't able to record their parts of "Tell Him" together, but you'd never guess that by the perfectly balanced recording.

"They're two of the greatest, if not *the* greatest, female vocalists of our time. To have your instincts match perfectly even though you're not together shows supreme musicians are at work. I think it's one of the most beautiful songs I've ever heard," producer Walter Afanasieff says.

After the song was finished, Celine anxiously awaited Barbra's reaction, and when it came, she cried so much

that Rene had to take the phone. But once the anxiety had melted away, her mood changed. "She was running around screaming, 'Oh my God! Oh my God!' like a little kid who just got a call from Babe Ruth about baseball or something. It was phenomenal. She was so thrilled," says Walter.

It took seven weeks for that album to reach Number One in the first week of 1998. That made it Celine's fastest-rising album yet. And to think, she almost turned down the biggest song of her career: "My Heart Will Go On," recorded in the spring of 1997 for the *Titanic* soundtrack, and released simultaneously on *Let's Talk About Love* (November 18, 1997).

James Horner and Will Jennings had written the song, but director James Cameron was intent on not having a "theme song" for *Titanic*. Horner thought the director might just need convincing, and he knew just the woman for the job: the singer he wanted to work with years earlier on *An American Tail 2: Fievel Goes West*. How far she'd come since then! He thought if he could get Celine on board, it might help.

Celine wasn't sure she was thrilled with the song and

ABOVE: In the studio with Sir George Martin and Carole King in 1997 for *Let's Talk About Love*. **RIGHT:** With Sir George after a performance.

TOP AND RIGHT: Preparing to sing "My Heart Will Go On" at the Academy Awards: the Michael Kors dress designs; the "famous" necklace; her ticket to the show. **BOTTOM:** With James Horner and Leonardo DiCaprio at the *Titanic* premiere. **PREVIOUS:** In the studio for *Let's Talk About Love* with the Bee Gees.

even signed a virtual "thumbs-down" to Rene after hearing Horner play it the first time. But Rene was enthusiastic—so enthusiastic, in fact, that he suggested that Celine should sing a demo version that he could take to Cameron. Celine rolled her eyes—what was her husband getting her into?

Horner would never have had the audacity to ask her to record a demo, especially considering the song hadn't even been approved, so he was thrilled by Rene's offer, and he began telling them stories about the tragedy of the *Titanic* and the characters in the movie, about Jack and Rose's love . . .

That changed everything. Celine listened to the song again and was able to hear what Rene had loved about it; she heard its potential, its heart-wrenching emotion. So with no reassurance that the song would ever be included in the movie, she recorded one take. That "one-take demo" became the song's single; it was so perfect that it was never rerecorded. The orchestrations were added later. And when people began to question Celine's attaching herself to a movie that was being talked about as a disaster worthy of its title, "They didn't care about any of that," says Paul Farberman, a business consultant for Celine and Rene's CDA Productions. "We saw a longer version of the movie in advance. They were crying. They loved the story, they loved the song, and that's all that mattered."

There was a giddiness about Celine while she worked on *Let's Talk About Love*, as if she were in the center of a grand fireworks display and almost carried off to the sky with it all. She had just won Grammy Awards for Best Pop Album and Album Of The Year (*Falling Into You*), and Diane Warren's "Because You Loved Me" won Best Song Written Specifically For A Motion Picture Or For Television. She teamed up with producer Sir George Martin, she finally got to sing with Barbra Streisand, and fan letters poured in to the tune of three thousand per week to the Canadian fan club office. She couldn't imagine what she would ever do to top this, and she was overwhelmed by the fan support.

"Can you imagine me opening all my letters, writing with my hand, answering everyone, singing, worrying for everything? It would not be possible," she says. So the Toronto office staff began reading all the mail for her. They still pass along the emotional requests and the touching stories, which she loves to hear.

Celine signs hundreds of autographs every week, often while she's having a massage or beauty treatment done. Doing this isn't any pressure for her, she says, and she does the best she can in trying to keep up. Signing her name doesn't take a lot of effort, but "it could mean a lot for them, so that's why I do it," she says. Of course, many fans ask for things that she can't fulfill. A groom-to-be will write, "My fiancée is Celine's biggest fan. Will she come sing at our wedding?" Even if she can't meet these requests, she's still happy to be asked. It means she's made a connection with fans, that they feel they know her and want her to be part of their lives. When she can, she sends photos and notes of encouragement to people whose stories have touched her—simple notes like, "Be strong. I'm with you. Love, Celine x x . . ."

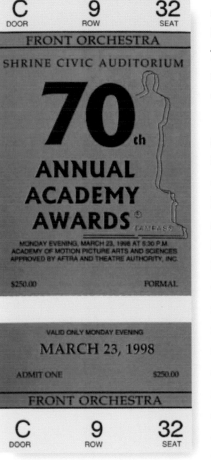

ALTHOUGH CELINE ENJOYS RECORDING, BEING on stage is her true love. Like most artists, she does get jittery backstage sometimes, but once the lights come up, the fright melts away. "I've never seen confidence like that,"

FALLING INTO YOU TOUR STICKER, JUNE 22, 1997

One of Celine's great international hits was the album *Falling Into You*, released in 1996. The album was full of songs that have become Celine standards in the years since its release, including "It's All Coming Back To Me Now," by producer John Steinman; "Because You Loved Me" (the theme from *Up Close & Personal*), by Dianne Warren; and "All By Myself," produced by David Foster. The album went on to sell 29 million copies.

The "Falling Into You" tour was equally wide-ranging, taking her all over the world. In addition to the U.S. and Canada, she made stops in Australia, Japan, and throughout Europe on the European Stadium Tour. Everywhere she went, she was greeted by enormous audiences. Her next English-language album would be *Let's Talk About Love* and include the theme to *Titanic*, and any lingering questions as to whether Celine had made it would be blown out of the water.

GRAMMY NOMINATIONS, FEBUARY 26, 1997

Celine won her first Grammy with Peabo Bryson for their duet on "Beauty And The Beast" in 1993. Four years later, she was nominated again, and this time on her own. The raging success of *Falling Into You* continued, bringing her nominations including Record of the Year for the single "Because You Loved Me (Theme From "Up Close & Personal")," produced by David Foster, and Best Pop Album for *Falling Into You*.

Your Category and Nominations

February 26, 1997

Category 01

Record Of The Year

This category is for commercially released singles released for the first time during the Eligibility Year, or for tracks from a current year's album. Award to the Artist and the Producer if other than the Artist.

1. **GIVE ME ONE REASON**
   Tracy Chapman
   Tracy Chapman & Don Gehman, producers
   Track from: New Beginning

2. **CHANGE THE WORLD**
   Eric Clapton
   Babyface, producer
   Track from: Phenomenon - Music From The Motion
   Picture (Various Artists)

LOVED ME (THEME FROM "UP CLOSE &

der, producers

The Infinite Sadness

says Dave Platel, "When you know everything that you're doing is great, and even if you make a mistake, you can recover with greatness."

He tells a story about the *Let's Talk About Love* tour to explain what he means. At the end of the show, she had gone off to make a costume change. Each night, when she came back, an elevator at the center of the stage would rise, and when the platform stopped, she would step out and sing. But one night, the elevator didn't work. So in her exquisite evening gown and high-heeled shoes, with microphone in hand, Celine gathered her dress in her free hand to climb her way up and out of the elevator and didn't miss a beat—she emerged singing "Every night in my dreams . . ." as if nothing had gone wrong.

She often tells her audience that the stage is home to her, that she is so comfortable she could sleep there. One of the reasons for that is there's no one she has to answer to once the show starts. If she decides to throw in a dance move or use new phrasing on a song's line, no one's going to stop her.

That's different from what it's like in the recording studio, where it's a group effort and many people are directing her. She may have sung twenty-two takes of the same song, but if someone at the record company decides he doesn't like one note, he can make her go back for a twenty-third take. Celine is involved at every stage nowadays; she even likes to sit at the boards and work on mixing her songs, but there's a lot of discussing and consulting going on with producers, engineers, and executives.

Producer Walter Afanasieff says Celine is "extraordinarily professional," a real rarity among recording artists. When he works with her, he knows there will be no surprises and no headaches. "She practices and practices before she shows up to the studio. She has a lot of respect for the producer and an incredible amount of respect and caring for the staff in the studio. A lot of artists don't even care enough to learn the song before they come into the studio. They have such a 'full of themselves' attitude—a lot of singers think that they just need to walk in and somebody's going to teach them the song and fix their voice; they only have a couple of hours to give, and off they go. Celine is the opposite: She's the consummate professional."

When she's in the studio, she doesn't want to waste anyone's time. She doesn't run off and make phone calls, do interviews, or try on outfits between takes. And she's always willing to listen to suggestions and work on trouble spots, like her accent—she's sometimes concerned about sounding "too French" when she sings in English. "It's beyond easy to work with her, not just because she has the most lovely and incredible voice, but because she gives one hundred percent," says Walter.

S'il Suffisait D'aimer was Celine's next album in 1998, again with Jean-Jacques Goldman, and Erick Benzi. The reunion was a special one for Goldman. "She's a little girl from Charlemagne, and I'm a little boy from Montrouge. She likes to sing, and I like to compose songs. That's all," he says. "She doesn't need to work with me, and I don't need to work with her, so we work together because we are happy to do it."

With that album, Jean-Jacques believes they've made their masterpiece, and doesn't think he has more to offer Celine musically, though they remain good friends. His one wish is that her English-speaking fans could understand her French lyrics. "I think that what she sings may be a little bit different, like in the song 'Le Ballet.' French audiences concentrate on the lyrics." This album, too, was a critical and commercial success, selling 4 million copies.

S'il Suffisait D'aimer was followed by *These Are Special Times*, a Christmas album on which she earned her first writing credit for "Don't Save It All For Christmas Day."

In 1998 Celine also hosted the Gala de l'ADISQ, at which the Felix Awards are presented in Quebec. She wanted to make a big entrance, so the crew put together an impressive opening act. The opening song was "Terre (Earth)," so the crew built a big wire mesh dome for her to ride in on from sixty feet in the air. During sound check, lighting designer Yves "Lapin" Aucoin told Celine she should practice the stunt once. He showed her that there was a metal bar for her to lean on and a safety belt to strap her in.

"I don't like the safety belt," she told him.

"Yes, but I prefer you to wear it," he said.

"Lapin, is it safe?"

"Yes, it's safe."

3

THE COLOUR *of* MY LOVE

"If I go and see a show, if I'm tired, I'm not going to

sit in the first row! I would stand there, my eyes open big, and

I would go, 'You go, girl,' and when they look at me,

I WOULD PUT MY THUMBS UP TO ENCOURAGE THEM.

I would come out of the show more tired than the

artist. I would breathe with them, I would dance for them,

I would hold my breath with theirs."

"SHE'LL SIT RIGHT DOWN ON THE FLOOR AND TALK TO PEOPLE. IT'S VERY EMOTIONAL FOR ME WHEN YOU REALIZE THIS LITTLE BOY HAS LEUKEMIA, AND THIS IS THE MOST IMPORTANT THING IN HIS LIFE—SEEING CELINE." —PATRICK ANGELIL needs a boost. "It's part of what helps me to go on doing the show," says Celine. When she meets someone who touches her, she remembers he or she is in the audience, and she wants to sing her best just for that person. That's who the show is for.

Before the meetings, Celine always wants to know about the child's illness, but she also wants to know about the child's hobbies, likes and dislikes . . . anything she can find out to have a better sense of who the person is aside from his or her disease. The child is allowed to come with his or her family—they all get tickets to the show and a chance to meet Celine beforehand and take pictures. Sometimes it's just a parent and child, but sometimes there are brothers and sisters as well. And if the child has special medical needs, a professional may accompany them. Celine wants to make sure the child feels special from the moment she walks in, so she asks Talia to identify him or her.

"I will tell her, 'Kimberly is wearing this and she's sitting in this chair,' so that she'll walk in and go straight to that child and say, 'Hi, Kimberly!' It's amazing because the child is so shocked that she even knows her name."

The staff loves to watch children's reactions. One of their favorite stories involves a five-year-old who came with her single mom for a meeting. The girl had a lung disorder and was hooked up to an oxygen tank. When Celine came in the room, the girl forgot she was hooked up to the tank—she ran across the room with arms outstretched to give Celine a hug and the tank got caught on a chair. Everyone was able to laugh about it, and it exemplified just what Celine hopes the children will get out of these meetings: a chance to forget about their illnesses for a while.

The girl got her own bodyguard for the night, too—Celine asked her guard Nick to escort the little VIP to her seat. The staff couldn't stop grinning as they watched Nick walk her to the ladies' room, then saw her peek out in amazement that he was still there. She grasped his hand tightly as they walked through the crowd.

When they're together, the children expect to ask Celine questions. But they're often surprised when Celine wants to hear all about them, too. She asks how they get along with their brothers and sisters, or what they like to do at home. She's a great listener. And she likes to give them gifts before they go.

But it's not just children whom Celine meets. There are similar organizations for terminally ill adults, and sometimes these are the most touching stories of all.

They blocked out a whole night for a woman in her thirties who was dying of breast cancer. She brought her husband and three young boys, and Celine says the woman taught her so much about strength of spirit. Normally, no video cameras are allowed backstage or in the theatre, even for the wish recipients, but they made an exception this time. Starting when she was diagnosed with breast cancer, the woman had been making a video diary so her sons would have a way to remember her. The meeting with Celine, her dying wish, became one of the last highlights on the diary. The woman passed away about two months later.

THERE'S A VERY PROTECTIVE QUALITY ABOUT many of those around Celine. They show a great deal of concern for her, and not just because of their job descriptions. It's as if they all realize Celine would overextend herself to the point of exhaustion if they didn't act as mediators. This is less surprising in light of the fact that most of the team has been around since Celine was just a teenager. Many of the staff members literally are family; the others are family in spirit.

Of course, there have been reasons to feel protective: Some fans are so obsessed that they'll do anything to meet her, including lying about having terminal illnesses or inventing sick children.

Then there are the few unexpected bombshells—like when a mother with two girls turned to Celine during the meet-and-greet and asked Celine to adopt the family. Or when Celine cancelled shows after her father's death and a very bitter mom wouldn't stop complaining about it when her child got to meet Celine a month later.

Thankfully, these occurrences are rare. More often, Celine walks away from these meetings knowing that she's just made someone's day, knowing that she had an impact on a person who may not have long to live. Sometimes, when the child is unable to come to the show, Celine will make a personal

---

LEFT: At Sainte-Justine Children's Hospital in Montreal, the beneficiary of many of Celine's fundraising efforts, 2002.

visit or a telephone call. She considers it all a great honor.

"She's very generous," Patrick says. "She'll sit right down on the floor and talk to people. It's very emotional for me when you realize this little boy has leukemia, and this is the most important thing in his life—seeing Celine. He has two more months. That's it for him."

You won't hear much about these personal meetings in the press. That's the way Celine and Rene want it. "Sometimes they ask us, 'Do you want a journalist present?' and we say no. You don't get the same reward," Rene says. He's amazed by how human his wife is; how well she can speak with people who are dying.

OF COURSE IT'S ABOUT KARINE. OF COURSE she can see Karine in every one of these children.

Karine was Celine's beloved niece, daughter to her sister Liette. Born with cystic fibrosis, doctors had not expected Karine to live more than a few weeks, but she made it to age sixteen, struggling all the way. Celine and Karine were particularly close, and Celine had always vowed that they'd find a cure. The two appeared on public service announcements in Canada when Celine was a teenager, and Celine became the national celebrity patron of the Canadian Cystic Fibrosis Foundation just after Karine died in 1993.

When Celine and Rene arrived on Karine's last day, she was on morphine and talking about everything running through her mind—her mother's cooking, new pajamas. It was Sunday and the stores were closed, but Rene convinced a manager to open a store so he could buy Karine new pajamas and nightgowns. He thought she knew she was going to pass away and she wanted to look good.

Celine lay behind her. "I was holding her and I started to sing her 'The Birds Of Happiness.' It's an Eddy Marnay song that came to me, and I was singing in her ears while my mother massaged her swollen feet."

After Karine's mother left the room, a tear ran down the girl's cheek, and Celine says she could feel every organ of Karine's body leaving one at a time. She was gone.

TOP: In Modena at the benefit "Pavarotti & Friends" for his charity. BOTTOM AND RIGHT: A recent benefit was a performance of "A New Day . . ." for victims of the December 2004 tsunamis, which was hosted by Larry King and raised more than a million dollars. Souvenir books included this note from Bill Clinton.

WILLIAM JEFFERSON CLINTON

April 20, 2005

Hillary and I are pleased to send warm greetings to everyone attending this special Mother's Day performance of "A New Day" by Celine Dion. We are grateful that you have chosen to use this occasion to support the children and families whose lives were devastated by last year's tsunamis, and we can certainly think of no better way to celebrate Mother's Day than by dedicating ourselves to the children of the world.

On December 26, 2004, one of the worst natural disasters in history struck Southeast Asia. The earthquake and subsequent tsunamis that occurred throughout the Indian Ocean that day lasted several hours, but its effects will be felt for years. Hundreds of thousands of people lost their lives, and millions lost homes, livelihoods, and sources of clean water and food. Tonight's special performance is an important way to keep those families in our thoughts as we continue to help them rebuild their lives and their communities.

Fortunately, people like all of you and my good friend Celine Dion are making it possible for them not to be without hope. By supporting this urgent cause, you truly are giving them a second chance at life. Although it still will be difficult to heal after a tragedy of this magnitude, your efforts will help us rise above the heartbreak and look toward a future full of promise.

Best wishes for a memorable event.

Bill Clinton

CANADIAN CYSTIC FIBROSIS FOUNDATION ANNUAL MEETING, 1997

Touched by the effect of cystic fibrosis on her family and the life of her niece, Karine, Celine has worked to raise money and support for cystic fibrosis research. In 1997 the Canadian Cystic Fibrosis Foundation, for whom Celine has done much of her work, honored her contributions at their annual meeting.

Celine's first work on behalf of the organization began when she was only fourteen years old, and she recorded her first public service announcement with Karine when Celine was sixteen. She has also personally supported the organization, donating a $290,000 appearance fee in 1997, asking guests of her 1994 wedding to Rene to donate to the foundation, which resulted in a pledge of more than $100,000, and of course sending large checks from her and Rene.

SPECIAL AMBASSADOR TO UNESCO LETTER AND SPEECH, DECEMBER 1999

In December 1999 Celine was named a special ambassador to UNESCO (the United Nations Educational, Scientific and Cultural Organization). She is the only Canadian and the first North American woman to be named to that position (of 65 nominees). The committee cited not only her tremendous success, but also her continued connection to her Canadian roots and her ongoing work on behalf of cystic fibrosis.

Among the dignitaries at the ceremony awarding her this honor was then-Quebec Minister of Culture and Communications Agnes Maltais. Agnes read the enclosed speech at the presentation, saying in part: "If only one song could bring peace to the entire world, I am sure Celine Dion would have sung it already. It would have been natural for her, since she has already sung of the power of love in many of her songs" (see translation, page 190).

After the presentation, Agnes forwarded the notes from the speech to Celine with this letter, which describes her as not only an admirer of her good works, but also of her music. Agnes writes that she was part of a performance group and sang "D'amour Ou D'amitie" herself (see translation, page 191).

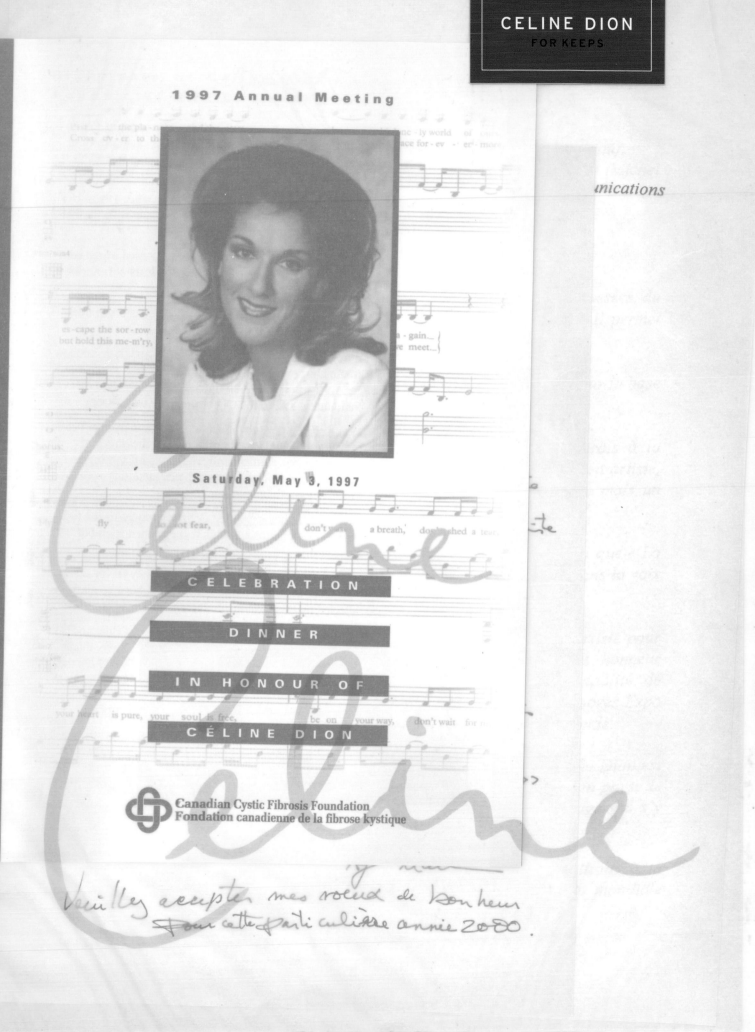

always a fan," says producer Walter Afanasieff. "No matter how big she gets, no matter who she is and how great she is, she's everyone's fan. If she runs into someone and she knows who they are, she wants their autograph. It's the coolest thing about her."

But Celine is quick to point out that while she may have *musical* idols, the person she looks up to most in the world has always been her mom, and her favorite song will always be the one Therese and Jacques wrote for her ("Ce N'etait Qu'un Reve").

"I cannot be more blessed," says Celine. "Singing is a way of expression for me and I can make my living with it—it's incredible. I can spoil my family. I bought my parents a house. I could afford for my dad, who passed, the prettiest bed and the most amazing flower arrangements. And clothing for my mother, renewing her new home for her to feel that, 'Okay, Dad passed and I'm home again.' I want to freshen things up for her, to say, 'Mom, do everything you want.' I'm capable of spending a lot of money for her to furnish again, and it makes me feel great."

All the joy and all the rewards that her singing has brought her don't get taken for granted. No matter what's going on in Celine's life, she never rests on her laurels and expects special treatment.

"When we recorded 'I Drove All Night' down in Miami, a few days before this, they found out her father had cancer," says producer Peer Astrom. "Two days before we recorded, she had a cyst explode somewhere on her body and she had to go to the hospital to get that fixed. The night before, they were filming a video out on a cold beach and she had a cold, and they were moving to Vegas the day after that, and we had to record this damn song. I don't know how she pulled that through. Anybody else would've said, 'Forget it.

Let's record another day. I hate this song. Get these people out of here!' But she has to give the music a chance. She's always about that. So even though she had all of this crap going on, no question about it, she was going to finish the song, and it was going to be good."

That wasn't the first time Peer saw Celine's tenacity. She had a cold the day they recorded "Naked" for the *One Heart* album, too, and she was feeling pretty lousy. There's an amazing high note toward the end of this song that would be difficult for most singers even on a perfect health day, but Peer and his partner Anders Bagge were praying that Celine would sing it. The singer on the demo had done it, and it blew them away. They didn't want to imagine the song without it.

"The people around her were trying to protect her voice again, saying, 'We don't need that note. Do something else. We don't like it anyway.' But Celine was determined—'I don't care. I'm going to do it!'—and she did it. We just yelled and started dancing around the studio. She's determined to do the very best she can every time. She's so much like a rock in her whole attitude. She wouldn't give up. It's her goal to

LEFT AND ABOVE: From her photo shoot for Chrysler in 2003, one of the many professional obligations she fits into her busy days.

24 Sussex

Mme Céline Dion

In honour of	En l'honneur de
Their Royal Highnesses	Leurs Altesses Royales
The Prince and Princess of Wales	le prince et la princesse de Galles
The Prime Minister of Canada	le Premier ministre du Canada
the Right Honourable Brian Mulroney	le très honorable Brian Mulroney
and Mrs. Mila Mulroney	et Mme Mila Mulroney
are pleased to invite you	ont le plaisir de vous inviter
to a dinner	à un dîner
at 24 Sussex Drive, Ottawa	au 24, promenade Sussex, Ottawa
on Tuesday, October 29th, 1991	le mardi 29 octobre 1991
at 8:30 p.m. for 9 p.m.	à 20 h 30 pour 21 heures

	Black Tie		Cravate noire
To Remind	Cocktail Dress	Pour mémoire	Robe cocktail

get whatever we want and for us to be happy with our song. It's very nice and it's very rare," says Peer.

Her kindness doesn't end in the studio. David Foster says that she and Rene are the kinds of friends you can count on. They don't get carried away with stardom. "It's over-simplification to say they haven't forgotten where they came from or who helped them get there, but they just are true to the people they care for," he says. "She's done so many things for me charity-wise for my own foundation, the Muhammad Ali event [Celebrity Fight Night], the concert for the Ronald McDonald House charity on World Children's Day . . . and I get requests for Celine every day. I don't take but five percent of them to Rene, but whenever I call him, I know he's going to say, 'Of course' and it's going to be easy access. I know it sounds too glowing, but there's just no bad news with them. They've lived their lives beautifully."

Sylvie Beauregard, who has been working as Celine and Rene's personal assistant since 1994, can attest to that beautiful way of living. In addition to running the office in Montreal as director of administration, Sylvie also takes care of a myriad of personal responsibilities for them. "Four years ago, Celine was in Montreal and had a morning appointment. I always ask the driver to call me when she leaves her residence so that I can inform the person with whom she has a meeting that she'll be there at a certain time. Early morning that day, my fifteen-pound dog, Mozart, was attacked by a larger dog as we walked in the park. A few minutes later, Johanne, the driver, called to confirm that Celine was on her way to her appointment. I was in a panic and explained that I was rushing to the vet because my dog had been badly bitten.

"When I got back to my condo four or five hours later, the doorman told me he had a package for 'Mozart Beauregard.' And there it was: a *huge* cushioned basket full of dog treats and toys, a blanket, a pillow, a bowl, a stuffed animal, you name it, it was there. The message read, 'Get well soon, Mozart. Celine x x . . . & Rene x x x.'"

Many friends also say that fans may not realize what a strong, powerful woman Celine is. She's not a complainer, and she has vast reserves of strength to work through the most nerve-racking times, like when she was asked to sing a second song at the Oscars in 1997 to fill in at the last minute when Natalie Cole got sick.

"It was panic time at the Oscars," says Rene. "I was there listening to the producer, who was trying desperately

---

ABOVE: Taking a punch with Muhammad Ali in 2004. RIGHT: With Sylvie Beauregard, Celine and Rene's personal assistant. PREVIOUS: Greeting one of the amazing women Celine has been honored to meet, Princess Diana, and the invitation to the prime minister of Canada's dinner for her.

to get another artist. I went to Celine right away and said, 'Would you be game to sing another song?' She didn't know the song, but it was a Barbra Streisand song, and she loves Barbra Streisand, so I said, 'If we go and buy the record right away and tomorrow you have a stand and you read the lyrics, can you do that?' She said yes. I went to the producer and said, 'I think I can solve your problem. What would you say if Celine sang it? He said to me on the spot, 'That's what I had in mind, but I didn't want to ask you because it's so difficult.'"

She learned "I Finally Found Someone" before she went to bed that night and performed it beautifully the next day.

Then there was the time when both her microphone and her earpiece failed during her 2004 Grammy performance of "Dance With My Father," a tribute to Luther Vandross. Grammy producer Ken Ehrlich asked Celine to sing it because she had recently lost her own father and he knew the song was a special one to her. Celine felt ready for it, and the dress rehearsal went off perfectly.

The live telecast, however, was a different story. First, no sound came out of her microphone and all the audience heard were nervous mutters from sound technicians in the control booth, then screeching feedback. The audience could see Celine mouthing, "It's still not working," and finally a technician ran out and handed her a new microphone. Richard Marx had already played the intro on piano three times, but he valiantly started again, and Celine began singing . . . then realized her earpiece wasn't working either, which meant that she couldn't hear the track.

She yanked the earpiece out and sang her heart out by memory alone, just trusting that she was on pitch and in time. Not only did she get a standing ovation, but her astounding professionalism and grace won over some of her toughest critics, who couldn't help but be awed by the way she pulled through.

Right after the performance, she jetted back to Las Vegas and performed "A New Day . . ." She had commissioned a comedian to entertain the audience during the half hour it took her to reach the stage. The ride there wasn't much fun, though.

"She felt terrible, terrible afterwards. She didn't say a word," says Rene. "She was so disappointed, and I think the people at the Grammys were as disappointed as she was. They sent her flowers, they wrote notes, but we don't talk about that anymore because I know that was not a good experience for her, especially because of what it meant to her to sing that song."

EVERY NIGHT ON STAGE NOW, CELINE SIGNALS upward with two fingers—her dad used to wag two fingers at people—and utters a quiet prayer while people are applauding: "Thank you, Dad. Come on, Jimmy, you can do it, baby." Jimmy is Celine's nephew, who was rendered quadriplegic in a skiing accident, and she believes her dad can help heal him.

Her dad is good at making his presence known, she says. On the day of his funeral, Celine's mom couldn't decide what watch to wear. They all seemed too flashy or wrong for the occasion, so she got emotional, gave up, and tossed them all aside. The following morning, she gathered the watches to put them away and almost fainted when she saw that every watch was stopped at 8:07—right around the time Adhemar had died. When Celine went to his room to say a final goodbye before going back to Las Vegas, she found his own watch, which had been removed in preparation for the funeral. It, too, was stopped at 8:07.

She says Adhemar mostly makes himself known to her through smell. Both of the last two years, when she was Christmas shopping, she felt like there was an invisible wall in front of her, and the smell of her dad's cologne. "You're here shopping with me, aren't you, Dad?" she asked.

Although she doesn't have a problem talking to her dad, she finds it very awkward to pray to God. *Did I do it*

right? Did I say 'please'? What if I forgot someone? Maybe it was selfish of me to pray for my family when so many people are dying, she thinks.

That said, Celine always enjoys being in church for the many family events she attends there: baptisms, weddings, funerals. "I think there's something very special about a church. When I come in to any church, I feel like lying on the bench and resting. The sound is so beautiful there. It feels like there's kind of an opening. I feel good. I think church can be inside of your soul, but I do admire the people who have time to go to church. Is it because they have the time or that they make the time? Is it because it's a need? But it impresses me. I hope one day I have time. 'It's Sunday, I'm going to church.' It sounds comforting."

When you go to church, she says, you can come in feeling empty and walk out feeling fulfilled, or walk in with too many burdens and leave feeling lighter and recharged. It's something she hopes to experience more as she claims more time for herself away from the spotlight. But she's always working on her spirituality, even when she's not part of a congregation.

"When I talk to my best friend, I always ask her, 'How is your spirit?' To me, spirituality is fixing everything that has to be fixed every day. I need to learn about that a lot . . . not holding a lot of stuff in, which I have a hard time with."

One of the traits she says annoys her about herself is that she always plays strong, even when she desperately needs to be cared for. Sometimes she wishes she could act like the "child-women," as she calls them, who act so helpless that a hundred people rush to their side when they get a fleck of dust in their eyes or complain of a headache. She, on the other hand, says that she could have a fever of 104 degrees and no one would notice because she'd say, "I'm fine, don't worry!"

"I'm my own problem," she says. "Some days I think I should just drop on the floor right here and play dead and freak them out. I'm dead! Then, when they bring me to the hospital, I'd say, 'Thank you for bringing me to the hospital. I needed compassion.'"

When stress gets to her, she finds comfort in playing with her son. Finger-painting, play dough, macaroni and cheese . . . these are the simple pleasures that melt her pressures away. She recently bought her first camera—a combination of digital and film that can snap one picture right after the other so she can capture every second when Rene-Charles jumps into a pool or plays golf. When magic happens, you can't ask it to hold on a minute while your camera resets. The photos are all over her house.

"If I don't stop, it's going to be wallpaper," she says. "The person who works at the house says, 'Who cares? It's your home.' You're so damn right! It makes me happy, so I'm putting pictures and more pictures on the walls."

4

BECAUSE *you* LOVED ME

"I don't necessarily want to have a perfect Godiva cake for my son's birthday. Once in a while, it's a rush, but when my kid was one year old, I made the cake. Cheerios were his favorite, so I put Cheerios all around it. I cherish that picture with that cake. **THAT WAS PART OF MY LIFE. I WAS PART OF HIS LIFE.** I was in control. It's very important to me, and it's a need, and I can't have it as often as I want it."

"I couldn't talk. It was like politics—avoiding questions and talking endlessly without saying anything," says Patrick. "We were constantly asked, and people didn't care about you, but they wanted to talk about it. I'm not selling records, I'm not on TV, but people want to talk to me because I'm related to her. It's like false popularity to try to get the gossip, but that's okay. When you're inside, you don't realize how big the picture is. It's just normal life for you; you don't realize how important she is to people who don't know you. Miles away from you, they talk and they're passionate about it."

Rene expected that that "passionate talk" could spell the end of Celine's career, but she was busting at the seams to tell the world, because she hated lying about such an important part of her life. Finally, she announced her relationship with Rene in the liner notes of *The Colour of My Love* album.

"We never had anything negative," says Rene. "I was very surprised . . . very, very surprised! I was certain that once it got out it would be against her, but on the contrary, ever since we went public, coincidentally, is the time when she started to be real big."

Producer Christopher Neil, who worked with them many times, remembers that even when he first met Celine and Rene, he thought they were so comfortable with each other. "It's a very odd thing to say now because at the time it was strictly manager and artist, but they were so good together even then," he says. "Years later, I was recording in Montreal and she came in and flashed this engagement ring at me. I said, 'My God, Celine, who is it?' because I had never seen her with anyone. She said, 'It's Rene.' I said, 'Wow,' and she said, 'What do you think?' I said, 'I'd marry Rene! He's such a nice guy, I'd marry him in a shot.' She cracked up laughing."

LEFT: With Rene in 1993, shortly before their storybook wedding. ABOVE: Adhemar Dion blesses his daughter before she walks down the aisle.

On December 17, 1994, at Notre Dame Basilica in Montreal, the lovebirds declared their commitment to each other in a fairytale wedding. The greatest surprise, Suzanne Gingue says, is that Celine cried even more than Rene did. He's usually more emotional than she is. She somehow lived through wearing the twenty-two-pound tiara that could have flattened her skull ("beauty before comfort" is her motto), and the wedding was televised in Canada.

They honeymooned in Florida, planning to take two months off, but soon after their vacation began, Dave Platel got a call from Paul Burger, who was Sony Music's U.K. chairman at the time. "Think Twice" was just going up the charts, and a big opportunity had presented itself.

"They have a huge TV show called *Top of the Pops* over there, and everybody tunes in to that show on Thursday nights to see the top artists in the world who are doing well in the U.K. charts," says Dave. "Burger called and said, 'We need Celine to come over and do *Top of the Pops*. Is there any sacred time?' Well, I called Rene and said, 'I have to make the call to you. I know you're on your honeymoon, very unlikely situation,' and he said, 'No, we can't go over there.'"

But fifteen minutes later, Rene called back. He and Celine talked about it, and she decided that the record company had worked so hard to push her album in the U.K. that she couldn't let them down when they finally had a hit and needed her. So in a span of three days, they jetted from Florida to New York, flew on the Concorde to the U.K., did the show, and flew back to Florida to finish their honeymoon.

Sometimes people assume that Rene, in his dual role of husband and manager, has control over Celine, but the truth is that she has the power to make her own career decisions; the control she's handed over to him has been done purposefully. She's not a meek, subservient woman. Politeness can be mistaken for meekness, and people can come to believe that her sweetness must be counterbalanced by his forcefulness. But even when she was a teen, those who knew her say they never saw any kind of Svengali stronghold. Rene, they all say, is a "gentle soul"; no one can remember ever hearing him even raise his voice.

Originally, Rene admits, Celine never went against his advice. "But as she grew older and wiser today, we have discussions. I suggest a lot of things, and a lot of times she won't agree. When she was younger, there was no discussion because she didn't know better. She knew that I had the experience, that I wanted the best for her, but now I understand that she has a lot of experience, and that she knows a lot of things about this business that I don't know. So, now we talk about it, whereas when she was younger, and she would come up with an objection, I would just convince her that I was right!" He laughs at the thought today.

ABOVE LEFT: Celine and the whole Dion clan at her wedding. ABOVE RIGHT: Rene kisses his bride.
RIGHT: The day after their wedding, Celine donned a second wedding gown, and Rene carried her over the threshold of their home in West Palm Beach, Florida.

In the roles of husband and wife, manager and artist, the lines do overlap. As husband, he wants her to rest when she's tired, to be pampered and relaxed, and never have to do anything she doesn't want to do. As a manager, he sometimes has to make decisions that are right professionally but less appealing to her on a personal level, like press meetings or business appearances.

"Even though she may not feel 100 percent up to doing a specific task, she recognizes that he's going to have her best interests at heart. She's a human being by saying, 'I don't feel like it, but I'll do it,' and that's a true professional," says Dave Platel.

And in return, Celine expects that meticulous work ethic and perfectionism from her staff. "At a TV show, she'll say to me, 'Will you check to make sure the sound guy has the right levels?'" Dave says, "and if the sound guy didn't have the right levels, she'll remind me about it later. She's very thorough. The details are important to her, and I learned to be on my toes as well. You can't bullshit Celine. . . . She'll make you crazy in a good way. She sets the bar very high, and unless you're up to the task, you're probably not going to be around too long. She's very demanding, but in a very gentle and reasonable way. I think that's a good combination."

ABOVE AND RIGHT: Celine arrived at her thirtieth birthday dressed elegantly. When she was surprised with a disco party, she quickly had to change to match her guests, including Rene's cousin Paul Sara (right) and her sister Claudette (center). Later, Celine was treated to a tour tradition—cake in the face.

CELINE AND RENE WEDDING PROGRAM, DECEMBER 17, 1994

Only a few short years after they announced their secret love to the public, Rene and Celine were married in a storybook ceremony and reception befitting their epic love story. Celine's headpiece alone weighed more than twenty pounds, and the lavish ceremony was described in this program handed out to guests (see translation, page 191).

CELINE AND RENE FAXES, JULY 1999

While on tour in 1999, Celine sent this fax from Amsterdam to Rene, who was recovering from his radiation treatments in North America, two weeks after their completion. Rene had called Celine earlier in the day, saying that he was feeling depressed, so she decided to cheer him up with some encouraging words. The fax, entitled "Swan Song," reads:

> From my window on high,
> Under a tearful sky,
> I seek in the waters of Amsterdam,
> The reflection of your face.
> As I look at the swans gliding by
> Erasing my fondest dream, to have you here with me.
> Come back to me, come back to me, she cries,
> Take me under your wing,
> And in the glimpse of a song
> They are gone
> In a sky of storm and thunder,
> And in a gust of wind,
> I will finally be back in the arms of my beloved.
>
> I miss you so . . . I adore you. Celine, Your wife xx . . .

Two days later, she sent this second fax from Germany. It reads:

> My beautiful bird,
> I wish I could be with you under your blue paradise sky.
> Here, alone under a cloudy European sky, I lose myself trying
> to find my way back to you.
> The flowers have no colors, chocolates never were so bitter,
> and even the wine is sad.
> I have only one thought: to be back in your arms soon.
>
> I adore you, your wife, Celine xx . . .
> P.S. My heart beats for you, regardless of time zone . . .

From the age of twelve on, she had been so focused on her music career that she ran herself ragged. And although her voice was strong as ever and her sales were astounding, she found herself quietly planning to walk away from it all for a while to find out what real life was about.

Originally, she planned to take a hiatus in 1997, but that was called off—partially because her record company, Sony, didn't want her to disappear at the height of her career and partially because she didn't get pregnant, as she'd hoped she would. While at times she told the media, "If it happens, it happens, and if it doesn't, it's okay," the truth is that she was heartbroken over the possibility that they might never have kids. They'd been trying since soon after the wedding, and it just wasn't working. Maybe because of all the stress and training, she didn't have regular menstrual periods, and she wanted to do whatever it took to give new life a chance.

More alarmingly to those who knew her, she had begun talking about her career as if it were a chore, something she never alluded to earlier. "I feel empty," she would say. Sometimes she envied her fans. She'd watch them at shows, standing with their friends, their husbands, and children, and realize that she never got to see life from their perspective. When was the last time she and Rene had sat in an audience just for enjoyment?

Many weeks she forgot what city she was in, spending just a day or two in one spot before taking a 2 a.m. jet to somewhere else. Marketing consultant Randy Irwin remembers that she fell asleep on his shoulder—while standing up—during the filming of the "My Heart Will Go On" video, after working for sixteen hours straight.

She barely slept, yet was expected to be friendly and perky everywhere she went. Who knew if a photographer was going to catch her in a half-asleep moment coming off a plane and plaster it on the front of a tabloid with a headline about a terrible drug habit, a twelfth miscarriage, or the ever-popular eating disorder?

Remaining "on" all the time was exhausting, even to someone with as much energy as Celine. And in more than a decade, she had never let up on her intense discipline: frequent periods of silence to rest her voice, avoidance of dairy products and carbonated drinks, even avoidance of laughter. It was always her goal (even to this day) to become a better singer.

To her, better meant that every performance had to be spot-on. Rene compares her to an Olympic athlete; the main difference is that athletes are in training for a limited time, then have time to rest. Celine kept herself under constant pressure to improve her talent, to the detriment of many other areas of her life.

Then came the most frightening thing the couple had ever experienced: cancer.

———————————

IN MARCH OF 1999, CELINE NOTICED A LUMP on the right side of Rene's neck while they were on an airplane. She figured it was swollen glands at first, but there wasn't a bump on the other side, and it wasn't tender, and it didn't hurt him to swallow. So, just to be safe, they called a doctor to do a check-up at their hotel in Dallas the next day. The doctor was alarmed enough to ask Rene to go to the hospital.

He did and had a biopsy right away. Celine had a performance to do; it was all such a blur that she can't remember where she performed that night, but she came back to the hospital to be with her husband as soon as she was done. Just before dawn, one of Rene's best friends, Pierre

Lacroix, told her to get some rest. He would stay with Rene.

But a few hours later, Pierre's wife Coco awakened Celine with the words, "Your husband needs you." Celine knew then that it was cancer. She didn't cry. Something inside told her that no matter what she felt, this was the time to be strong for him.

Rene was diagnosed with squamous cell carcinoma metastasic (a form of skin cancer). He had two surgeries the following day, and although doctors said they were able to remove all of it, they weren't taking any chances. Rene would start chemotherapy and radiation immediately.

"Why us?" was the question Celine struggled with. "We had it all . . . and maybe because we had it all that it has to be happening," Celine decided. "It's like a movie—it's so beautiful that it can't have a happy ending. When you watch a movie, if it's a sad ending, you're like, 'Of course she's going to die.' If it's a happy ending, you say, 'Of course it had to finish well.' People are never happy. It's always too sweet or too sad. So I said to myself, 'Our life was so marvelous. That's why I can't have a baby, because I have the most beautiful love in my life. I can't have a baby because I can't have it all' . . . or so I made up my mind. 'And he's sick because . . . because he's older, because I have so much success and something has to happen to me to balance it all out.'"

This time marked a major turning point for Celine. All along, Rene had been the strong one. He was the manager. Now everything had changed. "He was so weak, something that I didn't know from him. He was not the leader anymore. Of course I didn't want to see him weak and sick. But to see for the first time a man who loved me—which I had no doubt—but a man who needed me, a man who was lost, a man who kind of let go in me like a child . . . I was the manager. He reenergized my whole body and gave me the most important role of my life. Like, 'You're in charge. I need your help.'

"I wanted to cancel the tour and Rene wanted me to go on with it. It was one of the most difficult times for me in show business. He's the love of my life. I'm in charge. I want to give something back for him, and he says to me, 'I took so long to arrange the whole tour. If you're not doing

person." If you ask him about her worst qualities, he has to think much harder. "In the mornings, sometimes it takes time . . . it could take an hour before she wakes up. Me, I wake up right away. That's the only thing sometimes I have a problem with."

Truth is, Celine doesn't do mornings. She typically awakens closer to one thirty in the afternoon, and even then, she's dazed. That's why Rene didn't expect her to come to the hospital with him for all of his cancer treatments.

"When Rene went through radiation, I dressed up and made up my hair every morning," says Celine. "He wanted me to sleep. I said, 'No, I'm with you.' I don't think when you're sick you want to see someone look sicker than you, so I made myself pretty. I went with him to the hospital every day, and every day we passed in front of one of the busiest streets in Florida, and I could see water on the right and some grass and a bench . . . it looks like a park, but there was nobody there.

this tour, it's going to be harder for me.' I didn't want to aggravate anything, so I went and I sang my heart out for him. He could talk to me through my earpiece. I was responding to people, saying, 'Thank you so much for your applause,' and my husband was telling me, 'You are awesome. I love you' after every single song. He could see me live from the satellite at our movie theater at home. He was there."

Still, she couldn't wait to finish her obligations so she could be the wife she desperately wanted to be. Not a "showbiz wife," but a woman who really takes care of her husband.

If you ask Rene about his wife's best qualities, he has no problem listing all her positive attributes: "She's very honest, generous, sincere . . . that's why I liked her from the very start. She always tells the truth. She's like a child. I don't know how she could stay like that at thirty-seven years old, but I'm telling you she's a sincere

"There is a huge tree—I don't know what kind of tree, but it's gorgeous . . . very fat, very beautiful. I looked at Rene and I said, 'This is our tree.' I needed to give my tingling sensation, my rapid heartbeat, my bad stuff going on inside thinking I was going to lose him . . . I needed to push it out, and I said, 'This is our tree of hope. This is the tree of life.' Every day, we looked at the sun and the water and the tree . . . it was beautiful."

Before Rene began cancer treatments, doctors warned that he could become temporarily sterile, so they planned to freeze some of his sperm. Then they found out his sperm count was already too low for normal in-vitro fertilization treatments. Celine's obstetrician, Dr. Ronald Ackerman, suggested that they try a procedure known as intracyto-plasmic sperm injection, where one isolated sperm cell is injected into an egg, then placed back into the uterus. With Rene so sick and Celine on tour, they weren't ready

ABOVE AND TOP RIGHT: Celine and Rene count down the seconds to the new millennium, and to her long-overdue hiatus, at the Molson Centre in Montreal, December 31, 1999. **BOTTOM RIGHT:** Ticket to the Molson Centre concert.

TOP: With Roy Simkin and Dany Williams at Augusta National, two weeks before the Masters, in front of the famous 12th green, March 23, 1999. BOTTOM: Golfing with Annika Sorenstam at Le Mirage, the golf course that Celine and Rene own. RIGHT: With her best friend and Florida neighbor, Robin.

for Celine to get pregnant yet, so they put the plans on hold—waiting for the right time.

Then she announced her upcoming break. Some reporters declared that she was retiring, and many fans worried that she wouldn't come back. After all, she already had plenty of money and the satisfaction of major career success. The truth was more simple than that.

Rene's health had changed her perspective. Life was no longer a given. She stared into the eyes of this invincible man and realized he was human and fragile . . . and that meant that maybe she was, too. Did she want her entire life to be measured in trophies and platinum records? Did she want her career to be the central point of her marriage? Did she want to watch her ailing husband on a TV monitor from a stage in another city?

Certainly not. So Celine took a vow: She was going to teach herself how to be bored. She was going to learn how to be a normal human being who was allowed to wear sweatpants, have moody days, sleep in, rest when she was sick, and go to the beach on sunny days.

But if she was leaving the stage, she was leaving in style, so Rene planned a huge send-off concert for New Year's Eve 1999 in Montreal, where it all began. She performed for four emotional hours at the Molson Centre. Then, when the lights went down and the applause died out, there was . . . nothing. Nothing on the schedule book. Nowhere she had to be but their home in Jupiter, Florida.

———————————————

AT FIRST, SHE STRUGGLED WITH THE WHOLE concept of relaxing. Her entire life had been built around schedules, so she did what came naturally: She scheduled her relaxation, sometimes down to the minute. At 10:00, she would take a walk. At 10:30, she would read a magazine. At 11:15, she would go golfing.

The glorious transformation that took place didn't take long. Soon she tossed aside the schedule book and reclaimed her spontaneity. She didn't feel the pangs of work addiction tugging at her sleeves. She never wished not to set foot on a stage again, but she did relish her sanity break.

She'd never really had close friends before, but now she had that opportunity. Their dentist's wife, Robin, became her best friend after they discovered that they lived just two doors apart in Florida. Celine also became close with Annika Sorenstam, the pro golfer, whom she'd met in 1997 when Celine was in talks with Callaway golf.

Most importantly, she spent time with Rene. "The only thing we were doing is making love, playing golf, watching TV, movies . . . it was so simple and powerful," Celine says. "It was between life and death for about two years. It was my whole life, but today I can say only positive things even though Rene was very sick."

It taught her, rather quickly, that there was more than one goal worth pursuing in life.

———————————————

ALTHOUGH HE WAS NAUSEATED AND WEAK, Rene's treatments had gone well, and were complete in June of 1999. The following January, just after Celine's hiatus began, they celebrated the new millennium with 250 friends and family members by going to Las Vegas to see "O," the Cirque du Soleil show. Celine was mesmerized; there was so much to see on the stage. She tugged on Rene's sleeve and told him she wanted to do a show just like that. A show where it wouldn't just be her

standing alone on a stage and singing, but where she'd be surrounded by dancers and elaborate sets. A real visual experience for the audience. And Celine liked the idea of staying put in one spot for a while. It would give everyone on the team a chance for a more stable life. So Rene began to put the plans in motion.

By February, the couple felt ready for the next big step: Celine's fertility treatments. Just four months later, on June 8th, two elated doctors—one in person, one on the phone—let them know that the procedure was a success on the first try. Celine was pregnant!

Most people wait a few weeks before announcing a pregnancy even to friends because there's a high chance of miscarriage in the beginning. But Celine wasn't about to wait. She had been devastated when tabloids falsely reported she was pregnant earlier, and she wasn't going to give them the satisfaction of digging up her "secret" this time. It took her just one day to tell people on her

own terms. "We just found out yesterday afternoon, Rene and I, that the dream dearest to our hearts has come true," she announced in an official statement to the press on June 9, 2000.

She was as much of a perfectionist with her pregnancy as she was with her career. She gained fifty-five pounds and loved the way she looked and felt.

When she was eight months pregnant, she told her sister Linda and brother-in-law Alain that she wanted to take a weekend off and plan a special birthday for Rene on January 16, 2001. "I love to do picnics," she says. "We don't do that a lot. I said, 'I want to have a surprise. I will not bring him to a restaurant. I will not do a party, because I'm very pregnant, because I don't know if all the kids can come . . .' I just wanted to do something very intimate. I remember cooking all his favorite stuff. I called Rene's brother to talk to his wife, like, 'What spice are you putting in? How

ABOVE: Just starting to show, but Celine and Rene are already proud parents. LEFT: Rene and Celine celebrate the completion of Rene's cancer treatments at their Jupiter, Florida, home with a cake that reads, "Finished!"

"SHE'S VERY HONEST, GENEROUS, SINCERE . . . THAT'S WHY I LIKED HER FROM
THE VERY START. SHE ALWAYS TELLS THE TRUTH. SHE'S LIKE A CHILD.
I DON'T KNOW HOW SHE COULD STAY LIKE THAT AT THIRTY-SEVEN YEARS OLD, BUT
I'M TELLING YOU SHE'S A SINCERE PERSON." —RENE ANGELIL

long? How much?' and I wanted more recipes because I cook a little bit, but not a lot. I did so much food, and the prettiest stuff we had at home—cashmere blankets, gold plates, crystal—I brought it with us.

"But it took me so long to get dressed and prepare and everything—all the fruit and the décor, the Lebanese music, flowers that explode like fireworks with rose petals . . . It's beautiful, and he had no clue what was going on and where I was bringing him. I brought him to our tree of hope. It was supposed to be a brunch, but it took so long to pack and get ready that it was getting dark already! We were eating so fast. We took a few pictures—they're almost all dark—and we carved our message into the tree."

She won't tell what it means, but the letters they carved were L.V. It's one of the few secrets she doesn't share with the public, and it's a symbol Rene and she often sign to each other as a code of their love. They haven't gone back to the tree since, so she wonders if their carving is still there. Later, she learned from friends that they won't even drive past that street because it's one of the most dangerous neighborhoods in the area. That never seemed to occur to Celine; to her, it felt like a sanctuary.

Rene-Charles was born nine days later on January 25, 2001, by caesarean section after nearly fourteen hours of labor in which he refused to budge.

Before his birth, Celine had dreamed that if she had a boy, he would be a bit cold and indifferent to her. But she quickly found that her son was just the opposite: on the clingy side, affectionate, and a mama's boy.

"He has a strong personality," says Rene. "He's superstitious, like us. When he wakes up in the morning, as he passes he always touches the same things, he wants to do the same things the same way. If you tell him about a story and the next day, you tell the story and there's a little change, he'll tell you right away, 'No, no, no.' He's incredible, but he's our child; of course we're going to say that . . . but he is!"

At a year and a half, Rene-Charles started playing golf with his parents. Callaway designed little clubs for him, and he already has a straight, strong swing. He hits a ball, then chases it down and hits it again. He also has a fascination with cars. When guests come over, the first thing he wants is their keys so he can start their cars.

ABOVE: Nine days before Rene-Charles was born, Celine gathered some family members for a special picnic for Rene's birthday on Januray 16, 2001, at their "tree of hope." **LEFT:** Celine's precious pregnancy was one of the happiest times of her life.

RENE-CHARLES ULTRASOUND, NOVEMBER 27, 2000

One of the proudest moments of Celine's life was when she learned, after much effort, she was pregnant with her first child. On hiatus from performing at the time, she was able to focus all her energies into a safe and healthy pregnancy. Her rewards along the way were the first pictures of her new baby—in utero. This ultrasound from two months before Rene-Charles's birth shows him as a very happy and safe baby.

RENE-CHARLES BIRTH ANNOUNCEMENT, JANUARY 25, 2001

When Rene-Charles was born, it was the cause of much celebration for Celine's family, friends, and fans. Here was the perfect baby that Celine and Rene had wished for for so long. Like any doting parents, they had him photographed (by Anne Geddes, who would later collaborate with Celine on the *Miracle* book and CD project) and created this birth announcement/thank you note for all their well-wishers. It is clear from the images they selected that they are already doting parents only a few months after his birth. In one picture, Rene-Charles stands in a corner. Celine's father, Adhemar, had told her that when she was two and a half months old, she had the unusual trait of being able to stand in a corner. When Celine tried it with Rene-Charles, she found he shared this trait with her.

FAMILY PHOTO ALBUM

One of Celine's favorite things to do since Rene-Charles's birth is to take lots of pictures of him—and frame them for placement all around her house. This album includes some of Rene and Celine's favorite pictures of their son as they grow, laugh, and learn together.

people sang "Happy Birthday," hated photographers and applause and crowds and fans who would try to get Mommy's attention, and in particular, had almost a morbid fascination with a book that consistently made him cry.

It was one of those books with a play keyboard built in, where the child presses the buttons to hear notes. Rene-Charles would sit by himself with his book and press the keys . . . then cry—not just a few tears, but a full-on, chest-heaving, puffy-faced cry. Celine tried to hide the book from him, but he wanted it. He wanted to play those notes, but he wanted to cry every time he did.

Celine felt helpless—how could she stand to let her little boy cry? She went to his pediatrician, who said, "You're very lucky. Your son is doing his own therapy."

Maybe, the doctor suggested, Rene-Charles could feel just how much Celine was tormented by the idea of returning to music, and it hurt him as well. By playing his keyboard, he allowed himself to release those emotions.

That was it. Celine decided to fight for "the right things" and asked Rene to cancel the contract for the show she'd so desperately wanted in Las Vegas only a short time before. If it cost $50 million to buy herself out of the contract, she was prepared to pay it. She went to him in tears, begging him to work things out. But he couldn't.

Conflicting thoughts surged through her mind: She was stuck in a promise that she made before she knew her life was going to change so drastically. Soon, she would have to go back to being Celine Dion again—the smiling woman in magazine photos, the one who was supposed to perform every night and record, do promotional tours and TV specials, sign autographs, shoot videos. How could she have known when she set this dream at twelve years old that she'd one day feel a need to be "owned" by her child instead of fans?

Slowly, her panic eased as she got ready to rehearse for the show. She had made a decision: If the time came and she still felt wrong about doing it, she would cancel the show, no matter how it had to happen. This tug-of-war couldn't go on forever; if her career were on one side, and her son on the other, the winner would be obvious.

"I felt every day my son was telling me, 'Press the book. Press on the emotions in my heart.' He knows. Only him. How am I going to do this? Am I going to go against me, am I going to go against him? I went for a search and I pressed the book with him. He pressed the book, and I went by his side, and I didn't question. I said, 'I know.' I said, 'You know, Mommy cries sometimes when I hear music. Sometimes it makes me dance, sometimes it makes me laugh, sometimes it makes me cry. If you want to cry, Mommy's with you,'" she said.

But time fixed things, she says. It gave him room to settle inside and accept what was about to happen. And that allowed Celine to accept it, too. She never had doubts about wanting to sing again, but she didn't want to enter a world that would swallow up her son and take away the attention he craved so desperately from her.

So she took her first tentative steps toward the stage again. It was going to be the show of her dreams, after all, and she loved the people she worked with. They'd be in one place, and she'd be with her son before and after every show. Maybe it wouldn't be so bad.

Over time, Rene-Charles got better with crowds, better with attention. But she still felt pangs of guilt until her son gave her the best present of all.

It was her birthday, and until that point, she'd have to cover his ears whenever people sang "Happy Birthday"—he cried through the music, the crowds, the days that were supposed to be happy but instead were too overwhelming for him. Celine thought he associated birthdays with show business.

But on this birthday, her son sang to her. "I had anticipated that moment. That day was a whole life for me," she says.

They blew out the candles together, and from that moment on, she felt everything improved. The show would go on, but it was not going to be her main focus anymore. She would learn to put it in perspective, to get back in touch with everything she loved about singing without letting the pressures consume her.

These days, when she wants to relax, she'll hop into a bubble bath and turn the lights off. She doesn't have to worry about jet lag and hotel rooms. And she's consciously decided to be less fanatical about protecting her voice.

RIGHT: At Rene-Charles's second birthday party at home.

"I KNOW IT SOUNDS CUCKOO, BUT I BELIEVE THIS SO STRONGLY. I DIDN'T WANT TO
COME BACK TO SHOW BUSINESS, BECAUSE I DIDN'T WANT TO MISS OUT ON HIS SMILE, HIS WALK,
HIS LIFE. MY SON FELT ME, THAT I WAS GOING AGAINST MY FEELINGS." —CELINE

TOP: Celine, Rene-Charles, and Celine's sister (and Rene-Charles's godmother) Linda Dion prepare cupcakes together. BOTTOM: The family enjoys Easter together.

She wouldn't go to the other extreme and be reckless about her voice, of course. When she laughs, for example, no sound comes out. She demonstrates laughter by slapping her thigh, covering her mouth, or even literally rolling on the floor. It wasn't tough for her to learn to do this; she says she doesn't know why, but she could just switch off the sound pretty easily. It's just a habit now, not something she does purposely.

Every night before a show, she still does her vocal exercises, but not on her days off. After shows, she sings scales to "cool down." And she tends to speak softly and drink plenty of liquids to keep hydrated in the dry desert air. Rarely does she walk through the smoky casino.

The first year in Vegas went fast, and she found so much to love about this new project. This was the pinnacle of performing, in her mind—the dancers, the costumes, the sets. Her son often waits for her backstage. Only once did he react badly when he saw part of a rehearsal where dancers lifted Celine off a piano and brought her to the ground. She says, "He started to shake like crazy, and I said, 'They didn't hurt me, honey. They were just dancers trying to help me get my balance. It's okay. Mommy is not going to do that again.'"

Together, they came to an acceptance. She still craves a life with fewer schedules and responsibilities, but she has also found happiness here. "I love what I do. I don't regret. Regret and boredom are states of mind," she says. "Either one can make you crazy if you let it, or you can choose to find joy and excitement in your daily life."

The audience reactions help her tremendously. When she sees someone in the audience get emotional or jump up to dance, she remembers why she's doing this. "When I sit down and I say, 'This next song is for all the children and parents in the world, especially my son,' and I start to sing . . . there was a couple tonight in the first row and they were crying. I thought, 'Did they lose a child? Are they missing their child?' I sang the song for them and they didn't know it."

The extreme reactions excite her, too. When she takes a final bow and the audience remains on their feet clapping and screaming for five minutes, she adores how luxurious that feels.

About the only thing that could make her life better would be to see her family more often. Most of the family still lives in Quebec in the towns of Charlemagne, Repentigny, and Laval.

"Because all the brothers and sisters have their own families, it's not so easy for some to visit each other often," says Michel. "But for weddings, baby showers, or other special events, it's always a good reason to see each other. Of course, at Christmas, the whole family gets together."

For one week last year, Celine and Rene were able to be in Montreal for the holidays, for an intimate gathering of two hundred family members! Along with the brothers, sisters, in-laws, nieces, and nephews, many of the nieces and nephews even have their own kids now, and Rene's family comes, too. Therese insisted on cooking, and Celine said she'd hire help.

"Okay," Therese replied, "They can cut the carrot sticks, but I'm going to cook."

Celine loves spoiling her family for Christmas. Last year, Rene-Charles got a snowmobile that travels about eight miles per hour, and she says he was "freaking with happiness" when he got to ride it in their big backyard, wearing his snowsuit and helmet.

She likes to give each of the kids in the family a Toys 'R' Us catalog and have them mark all the toys they want. "Every Christmas, we get money and gifts," says Michel. "The kids get many, many toys in a fabric pouch and red ribbon with their names on it. Our bodyguards arrange to close a store for the general public, then Celine and bodyguards and helpers go in there and she says, 'Okay, I want six of these, three of these . . .'"

Celine's latest Christmas was even more of a shopping marathon because her staff has grown. "Why can't I just say, 'Oh, let's buy Tiffany frames this year for everyone and stick in a picture with my short blond hair'?" she asks. But she can't. It's too important to her to choose personal gifts for everyone.

"For example, my personal assistant, who dresses me and undresses me every night . . . I almost forget how to undress myself without her!" Celine was looking for a particular kind

ABOVE: Celine records with her whole family for a track on *These Are Special Times*.

of hatbox for her and discovered that manufacturers don't make boxes for large-brimmed hats anymore because they're no longer in style. It would have taken six months to have one made, but Christmas was coming in three weeks. So she cleaned her own hat box and gave it to her, explaining the story behind it. Anna DeMartino says that is typical of Celine. "Even with her schedule, she always has time to put a smile on people's faces. She remembers everybody's birthday—friends, family, staff—she makes sure she calls you or sends you something."

When Rene buys gifts for Celine, though, he likes to be tipped off, so he enlists friends to do detective work for him. When she's out shopping with someone, he wants to know what she was looking at, particularly if she commented on any beautiful pieces of jewelry. Then she's amazed when he picks just the right thing.

Sometimes, though, she gets special gifts that mean more to her than the fanciest jewelry money could buy. Rene says they have a tremendous stack of drawings fans have done for them. Sometimes, he says, it's lucky that they write the names "Celine," "Rene," and "Rene-Charles" under the drawings because they're not all exactly Rembrandts!

"I think it's the ultimate way to show your love," says Rene. "When you're a baby and you draw your mother, the baby wants to show how much he loves his mother. Rene-Charles tries to do that. So when we get these drawings, even though it's funny to look at some of them, the intention is incredible. It means that they love her so much."

Some gifts are even more personal. After years apart, Celine's mother reconnected with a childhood friend in 2004. "I never knew that my mother had a friend," says Celine. "It's very touching for me. When she told me she was going to come to Vegas, she asked me if she could bring that friend. They've come to see the show two or three times already in a week. Monique is such a funny character. I'm so happy she's here, and she brought me something. She said, 'It's a long story, but this belongs to you.' She gave me a miniature porcelain plate set, with a cup and saucer. This is the first set that my mother had. When my mom was five years old, she would play with it.

"Monique kept it for seventy-two years. It's impeccable.

I have a hard time keeping things for two weeks! I wasn't sure that I should take it, but my mom said, 'Sure, I want you to have it.' It's amazing. Sometimes I think I can get everything in the world, but you can't imagine how much this little plate meant so much to me."

But Celine is more giver than receiver. For many years, Celine has "adopted" families in Quebec over the holidays. She calls charity foundations to find out details of about five or six families each year who are in need, and she likes to go in person to bring presents and items they need. If they're too shy to meet her, she'll send things by mail. Rene's daughter Anne-Marie has followed this path, too.

This year, Celine decided to pass these values on to Rene-Charles. "I didn't push him, but I encouraged him," she says. "I said, 'Do you know how many cars you have? It would take us days to count them. Some kids don't have even one toy.' About two months before Christmas, I emptied his playroom with my sister Linda. We put all of the puzzles with the puzzles, all the cars with cars, all the teddy bears with teddy bears, all the blocks with the blocks . . . We took one box at a time, and I said, 'Christmas is coming and if you receive more toys, we would not have anywhere to put them, so let's make room.'"

She picked up each toy and asked, "This game—should we keep it or give it to a child who doesn't have any toys?" He was happy to be involved and let her know which things they could give away.

That made Celine happy, because as much as she likes to spoil and be spoiled, it's important for her to remember what matters in life, and she wants her son to grow up with the right frame of mind.

As Rene-Charles grows older, she's also sensitive about shielding him from adopting her pressures. Most four-year-old kids, she estimates, may get ten presents at their birthday parties. Rene-Charles gets more like a hundred. It's a fine line between teaching him manners and burdening him with social graces that a child shouldn't have to bear.

"I want him to be polite and appreciative of what he receives," she says. "On the other hand, I'm sorry, but I don't want my son to spend his whole day saying 'thank you.' I also

don't want my son to make seventy-five phone calls the next day, because what will happen is my son one day is going to say to me, 'I don't give a heck about my birthday. I'm so tired of all those people. You call them my friends? It's giving me a job. You're in show business, you know a lot of people, you do a lot of PR. This is my birthday. I want to be alone.'"

Just like when she was a little girl and playmates took her dolls, she now feels that some people believe Rene-Charles is supposed to be the model of generosity. Sometimes parents see no problem when their kids come over and take toys from Rene-Charles. He has it all, so he has no right to complain, right?

It was her choice to live in the spotlight, but he's a child, and she'll do anything to let him find his own way. She senses the same "old soul" quality in him that she feels in herself, but she has no desire to add responsibilities to his young life.

"When Rene-Charles was a baby and I took him in my arms in the rocking chair, breast-feeding him, very often my eyes got caught looking at him and him looking at me. I saw my soul. I saw my childhood. And there was a message: 'Mom, don't screw it up. Take care of yourself if you want to save me.'"

That's when she started taking a stand in all areas of her life. She got pickier about the types of songs she wanted to record, more adamant about her time off, and set "ground rules" about fans approaching when she was with her son. "Who makes the rules?" she asks. "We make the rules. I want to be the conductor of my own life. I can't hear young kids today who say, 'Singing is my life.' It kills me. I used to say it, but singing is not your life. What happens if you don't have a career—you don't have a life? So you can have dreams, you can have passion, but keep a place for yourself. It's a big price to pay," she adds, tears welling up in her eyes. "You certainly lose a part of yourself. People come to me and say, 'Do you know how many lives you're helping and changing?' Yes, but what about saving my own?"

ABOVE: Rene, Rene-Charles, and Celine in front of the fireplace as they celebrate Christmas 2004.

A NEW DAY *has* COME

"Would I be capable today to go back to work anywhere,

a normal job? Yes. It would be hard—it's hard

for everyone to have a job, five days a week, nine to five—

but I have my son, my family. I know that I would

not be capable of spoiling my family as much,

but I can go into a lot of things because I'M HEALTHY

IN MY MIND AND I'M HEALTHY IN MY HEART."

I SAT WITH MY FAMILY IN THE FORMAL DINING ROOM IN THE DRESSING ROOM AREA AWAITING CELINE'S ARRIVAL. IT HAS TO BE CALLED AN "AREA" INSTEAD OF JUST A DRESSING ROOM

because it's the size of a rather large house and contains an office, a living room, a kitchen, bathrooms, and a costume room, in addition to the actual room where Celine changes and has her hair done. *The walls are covered in suede*, I realized. Suede! Light gray, all throughout the dressing room area.

I was supposed to interview Celine after the show that night, but when her staff saw that I had my parents and little brother with me, they offered to let us take pictures with her beforehand. The problem was that it was now 8:20, and she was scheduled to be on stage in ten minutes. No way could she still make it, I thought.

But just in case, we all stood by the door, already posed and ready in case she was able to just run through and snap a shot or two with us. A minute later, a very tall woman in a stunning red dress rushed through the door waving her hands in the air and calling, "I'm sorry! I'm sorry I'm late!"

"I want to blame it on my hair," Celine said, "But the truth is I'm always running late." Her hair, flowing and layered into light brown waves, looked soft and touchable.

"Did the fans not like the short blonde look?" I later asked. She could hardly contain herself from imitating the horrified reactions she got from fans.

"'Celine, where are you? We trusted you! It's shorter and shorter, naked! You're changing things! You betrayed us!' I wanted to have my short hair because I wanted to give it a try. For God's sake, I'm a normal person, a girlfriend. I wanted to try how blonde is. I'm still the same person!"

The media was suddenly buzzing with attention on Celine's hair. Finally, she gave up and changed her hair back, but the questions didn't stop. Now they wanted to know why she changed it back.

"Because I'm tired of talking about my hair! Don't worry, my hair will be performing tonight," she says. "I could have seen it two ways: One is that I'm no more than hair, but the other is that they love me so much that they want me the

---

ABOVE: Discussing the moves with creator Franco Dragone. **LEFT:** Celine does her own makeup every night before "A New Day . . ." **PREVIOUS:** Surrounded by dancers onstage during the show.

way I presented me the first time. They want me back. It was like I was too edgy for romantic songs, the dreams and the long hair, the softness . . . that's the girl. I guess that long hair was, for them, something trustable. I think everything changes so much today in life, stability is very important as well, precious. Having an image they can relate to, something reliable, they could trust me for that . . . but when they saw my short blond hair, they thought I flipped. 'Now she's going to get naked in her videos! She's going to have her tongue in everyone!'"

As she stood there before us, it was hard to imagine that this was a woman who ever had any insecurity about her appearance. She's strikingly beautiful and appears much taller than the 5'7" I'd always heard. Perhaps it was her heels, but it was also her perfect posture. She stands with shoulders back, claiming every inch as her own.

She took the time to have a quick chat with each of us, asking my dad if he was the family photographer today, bending down to give my brother a hug. I was already conscious of the time: "She's supposed to be on stage in *five minutes*." But she wasn't going to let a sold-out concert stop her from asking assistants to take some shots so my dad could be in the pictures, too. After more hugs and kisses on both cheeks, she was finally off and literally running—and so were we. Just as we got to our seats, Celine appeared on

the stage before a sold-out audience, just as she has so many times since the show opened in 2003.

———————————

WHEN RENE FIRST PROMOTED CELINE, HE HAD to do a lot more arguing on her behalf than he does now. Still, he says, it's not just a given that Celine will get anything she wants.

When she wanted the show at Caesars Palace, Rene says, "They knew the power that she had to attract fans here because she has a track record of sold-out shows everywhere, and she had played here a few times and every time it was fantastic for them. But I still had to convince them, because it cost $95 million to build . . . so they wouldn't say yes on the first meeting, but I thought that they were pretty smart and pretty quick in understanding the whole project and going with it."

Indeed, Caesars built a special concert hall just for "A New Day . . ." The Colosseum, as it's called, has 4,100 seats and is equipped with the largest indoor LED screen in North America. The screen provides the backdrop for the show, at times looking like a Salvador Dali painting and at other times looking like a giant animated postcard.

The stage is sloped, with the far end of the stage the highest point, like a very wide ramp. The angle of the slope

ABOVE: The "A New Day . . ." team: Tom Gallagher, Park Place Entertainment; Rene; Celine; creator Franco Dragone; John Meglen, Concerts West; and Tim Leiweke, AEG Live.

gets more severe toward the back of the stage. This was Franco Dragone's idea; if the stage were sloped, he realized, everyone in the theatre would be able to see every person on the stage.

Then there's the $2 million humidity bubble. Warm, moist air is best for a singer, so Rene insisted that the theatre and dressing room be set up for optimal conditions. Wherever Celine is singing, the air is humidified. In front of the stage, if you look carefully, you can see steam rising from the vents.

As for her dressing room, Rene is proud to say it's probably the best dressing room any artist has ever had. Because all the requests were made before the building was constructed, they were able to build it to her exact specifications.

"You have to understand that she is going to be here for four years, five days a week, and she spends maybe six or seven hours per day here. It's very comfortable; it's perfect for her—everything from a massage room, a steam room for her voice, a personal dining room for herself, a kitchen where the cook prepares her dinner . . . "

She's taken to keeping many of her awards in the dressing room area. The living room displays her Ella Award and the

TOP: The Colosseum under construction. **BOTTOM:** Celine was a draw for Caesars long before "A New Day . . ." opened; this marquee is from two shows she performed in August 1996.

Woman of the Year award from the Nevada Ballet Company. But the focal point is the giant framed white poster in the center of the wall: Here, there are signatures and short messages from a number of celebrities who've come to see the show.

Oprah's message is center: "You make me proud to spell my name 'woman,'" it reads. "You make me weep with joy" is Neil Sedaka's message, Sly Stallone writes, "Keep singing—you're a champ," and Arnold Schwarzenegger writes—what else?—"I'll be back." Sir George Martin, Jean Paul Gaultier, Barry Bonds, Britney Spears, Michael Douglas, and Catherine Zeta-Jones are among the others who've signed the board. And best friend Robin, who doesn't include her last name, tells Celine she's always in her heart. There's no more room for signatures, so they've started a second board on the wall next to her elevator.

Celine arrives at the theatre at about 5:30, or a little earlier if she has a sound check to do that night. Once there, she meets with Suzanne Gingue, her former tour director; now that they're staying put, she's Celine's personal director of operations. She briefs Celine about what's going on that night.

TOP: With Sylvester Stallone, Rene, Michael Douglas, Catherine Zeta-Jones, and Caesars president Mark Juliano before a performance of "A New Day . . ." BOTTOM: Celine's good friend Oprah Winfrey, shown here in 1997, has also come to see the show.

ABOVE: Many of her VIP well-wishers have signed this board after visiting, and a second board is currently in rotation. This board features Rene-Charles's "drawing" for his mom at the bottom center.

Some nights Rene-Charles is in tow. That's why her personal dressing room is set up to feel homey and is filled with toys. It's the only room where there's not a constant buzz of traffic; few people come into Celine's room. It has its own key, separate from the rest of the already-secured area, and the bodyguards' station is right outside.

Sliding frosted glass doors mark the entrance to this large suite. Inside sit two big, gray leather sofas and an oversized coffee table covered by fashion magazines. The makeup area is a large lighted mirror flanked on both sides with dark oak bookshelves. On the shelves are biographies of legendary celebrities she admires, and they're an interesting bunch—Frank Sinatra, Coco Chanel, Rita Hayworth. On a bottom shelf is a little painted cow with a punk-rock hairdo, with the words "A Moo Day . . . " written on the side, a gift from one of the dancers.

Throughout the room, there are photos of Rene and Celine and Rene-Charles, along with photos of Celine's siblings and parents and friends. A beautiful mosaic of Celine and her father hugging hangs over a couch near the room's entrance.

There's also a bathroom and shower in here, and a walk-in closet. Several storeowners in the Forum shops will bring clothes or jewelry for her to try on, and because she's a night owl, she does this after the show.

Then there are fans' presents. All staff members are instructed to give Celine the letters and gifts fans have brought for her, so she really does see everything. Much of it winds up in the dressing room, at least temporarily. She stores fan gifts and letters in three warehouses in Las Vegas, Florida, and Montreal.

She has a massage room in the suite as well, where her physiotherapist, Rollande Savard Souliere, works her magic every night before and after the show. In 1998, when Celine was experiencing back pain, a doctor recommended she hire someone to give her ongoing treatments. When the doctor asked Rollande, who had worked for him for twenty-five years, if she knew anyone who could travel with Celine, she volunteered. For at least an hour after each show, Rollande gives her treatments to help her combat the strain of working on the sloped stage, which is very stressful on her leg

ABOVE: Celine signs an autograph for Mandy Gulbransen of Minneapolis, the lucky one-millionth fan who came to see "A New Day . . ." **RIGHT:** When the show began, Celine tried on many wigs to see if one might be right for the show—but ultimately decided to go with her own hair instead.

TOP: Celine with longtime tour director and friend Suzanne Gingue. BOTTOM: Rollande Savard Souliere administers Celine's daily electrotherapy treatments to keep her legs strong and healthy.

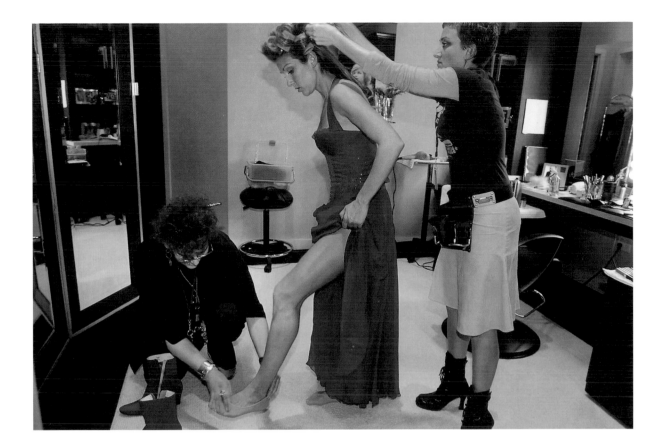

muscles. Electrotherapy helps to ward off the shin splints she was developing. It's hard for Celine to sit still and get this done—she's a ball of energy. She'd rather give massages than receive them, but she knows she needs these treatments to keep her body in shape.

In fact, she's had a few physical problems since starting the show. Once, a neck injury forced her to cancel a few performances. "The vertebrae were irritated and caused a lot of pain," says Rene. "Sometimes it comes back. We don't know if it's the show or maybe the training, because she trained for three months before she did this with the trainer of the Olympic team in Belgium. He's a very rigorous trainer, and she did things very hard to be in top shape. The doctor said maybe the training was too hard."

Many people assumed the neck injury was from the "flying" Celine did onstage; she was strapped into a harness and sang "The First Time Ever I Saw Your Face" while hovering over the stage. But actually, that was a different injury altogether. That one gave her a hernia. Now the flying

has been delegated to a dancer wearing Celine's costume. Celine also has body doubles who sometimes stand in for her during rehearsals. Celine continues to train to stay in shape for all the dancing; she's practiced yoga, and recently she has taken up Pilates.

Of course, then there are the miscellaneous illnesses that no one can predict or prepare for, and these scare Celine the most. Once, she had an asthma attack compounded by a panic attack onstage. "I was in Los Angeles on the most polluted day of the year. I sang there, then took the plane back, and I rushed here and was onstage in twenty minutes. I was nervous because I was dehydrated. I started to breathe faster, and the faster I was breathing, the more dehydration I felt. The more I pushed, the more I was out of breath." She exited stage right after "Seduces Me" and dropped to the floor. She cooled down and tried to sing more, but after six songs, she couldn't go on. "I dropped on my knees, and they had to open my dress. I was having oxygen in the back room, and the EMT workers and my doctor were here."

ABOVE: Celine dresses for the show with the help of hairstylist Tricia "Zhane" Jenkins and dresser Denise "Zorba" Soteras.

ABOVE: When the show began, Celine used to be raised into the air during one number. Due to some physical problems, most of that stunt work has been handed off to other dancers.

Another time before a show she was getting oxygen to combat breathing troubles when her body just seemed to give out. Her back, hands, and feet spasmed, she couldn't swallow, and everything turned blurry. "There was a bouquet of flowers in front of me. Everybody was talking to me, trying to get me to breathe because I was not breathing, and I remember on the left my husband saying to me, 'Think of Rene-Charles.' I think he thought I was going to die. Everything kind of disappeared, and I could not hear them. I only remember the bouquet, which seemed to get narrower and narrower." It took her three days to recuperate.

It's an awful load of responsibility to know that literally hundreds of people's careers depend on your throat. In Las Vegas alone, there are 164 people on staff—this includes the dancers, musicians, office workers, technical crew, assistants, beauticians, therapists, stage crew, wardrobe, and more. Then there are the people who work in CDA, Five Star, and Feeling Productions in Montreal, Toronto, Los Angeles, and New York.

Add that to the pressure of knowing that some people have saved up money for more than a year and had to apply for visas to travel from overseas to come to her show. If she cancels, she knows some of them won't be able to come back. "I definitely feel total responsibility. People have the right to feel very mad if the show was canceled at the last minute. But as a performer, I cannot say two days ahead of time, 'I don't feel so good, so cancel three shows.' It doesn't work like this. I can wake up in the morning and not feel so good, but I have to warm up, take medicine, put on the heat for breathing . . . maybe it'll be all right. I have to wait for the last minute, but I also have to be fair and give a show. I'm a singer—if I can't sing, what do you want me to do? Look pretty? It doesn't work. Dance? I'm not a dancer. I need my instrument and sometimes it doesn't work. The reality is that I have some asthma, I have some allergies, some sinus infections. These things happen."

When they happen, she says she doesn't care about feeling sick. What breaks her heart is that she knows what's going to happen in the theater. She knows some people will yell, some will cry, some will curse, and some will understand.

But most of all, she'll know that she let people down, and that's the last thing she wants to do. Celine has canceled very few performances since she began her Vegas show in 2003. Caesars president Mark Juliano adds that you know if Celine cancels, it's for a good reason. "It's not because she woke up and her left eyebrow was crooked," he says.

Indeed, if her eyebrow were crooked, she'd have only herself to blame. Every night, Zhane Jenkins comes in to do Celine's hair before the show. But she does her own makeup. Ying Yuang sets up the makeup table for her and cleans it every night, but Celine likes this rare chance to be alone before a performance.

Once she's ready and finished with any meet-and-greets she has that night, the monitor engineer, Daniel Baron, comes in to clip on Celine's microphone. Then she tells her brother Michel that she's ready to go. A bodyguard escorts her up her private elevator to the stage. She has some quirky superstitions that have multiplied over the years—she has to apply her deodorant a particular way and touch thumbs with the musicians before a show, for example.

But once on stage, all cares are left behind, and Celine focuses on connecting with her audience: the people who have traveled, sometimes across the world, to be with her in Las Vegas. She's always watching, making eye contact with the fans who have tears in their eyes. Listening to the audience's comments, responding when they shout, "I love you, Celine!"

It's the reactions that keep her from getting tired of singing the same songs night after night; even though she may have sung the same song a thousand times, it's the first time that many of the fans have heard her sing it, and it may be the last time. So she wants to make it special for them.

But there's a strange phenomenon she hasn't quite figured out: Most of the time when she's not in great shape and she feels like she's compensating vocally, the audience goes wild, but when she feels like she just performed at the top of her game, their reactions are mild.

"I feel like, 'Did you hear what the heck I did? That was incredible! That was awesome, Celine. You rock, baby. Let's try again.' And every time, when I'm tired out, puffy,

"A NEW DAY..." PREMIERE, MARCH 25, 2003

The opening of "A New Day..." was truly the beginning of a bold new endeavor for Celine. The project, which had been in the making ever since she saw a performance of Cirque du Soleil's "O" in 2001, marked a major departure from a life of performances on the road. Now, she would have her own "colosseum," four-thousand-seat strong and designed for perfect acoustics and staging. She would have a home away from home in her permanent dressing room. And she would have a place to raise her son in relative stability.

The show opened on March 25, 2003, to rave reviews. In less than two years onstage, the show had already sold a million tickets, and still plays to sold out shows more often than not. Projected to run through March 2007, it is constantly revised and updated, so the many fans who come to see it again and again are never disappointed.

SIEGFRIED & ROY AND MUHAMMAD ALI CONGRATULATORY NOTES

Of course, when Celine came to Vegas, she wasn't the first to have a semipermanent home there. Siegfried & Roy had been performing at the Mirage for years. After seeing the premiere of her show, the duo sent a note in admiration of her performance.

Muhammad Ali, who Celine knows and has performed benefits for, sent this note with a bouquet of flowers when "A New Day..." opened.

ABOVE: Brother Michel Dion and Celine both prepare for the show.

and just so sick that it shows, they go crazy, and I'm like, 'Are you laughing at me? Are you serious right now?' They're giving me four standing ovations. 'Okay, who is making funny faces in the back? Is there something coming out of my body that I don't know? Is it my new perfume that I'm wearing that they love so much?'

"Of course I compensated. My vocal cords—I almost threw them out, they came back, they slapped my face and went back into my soul. They see the pain, they see the effort. If you don't show them that it's hard, they don't react. Sometimes the simplest thing can be the hardest to sing, like 'Ammore Annascunnuto' while just walking straight on the sloped stage."

Rene sees the show about once a week now, but for the first six months, he was there every night. In fact, he says, he has been in the audience of every show she's ever given (except during his cancer treatments, when he watched via satellite) until now. But even when he's not in the audience, he's often hanging around near the theater, and fans approach him regularly.

"Most of the guys who come to see the show are being dragged by their girlfriends or wives," says Rene. "You don't have any idea of how many times every day somebody stops me and says, 'You know, I wasn't a big fan, but my wife and I went to see the show, and she's incredible.' My poker friends—imagine poker players, not necessarily their style to see Celine—would say, 'My girlfriend is bugging me for tickets because she knows that we play poker together.' Everyone I play with went one after the other, and they're all amazed. You have no idea until you see her performing live what type of artist she is."

When she's onstage, little can distract her. The dancers like to play jokes sometimes to see if they can get her to laugh during a song, but she's focused on the audience. She spots the people with their arms crossed in the beginning of the show, and if she can make them stand up and dance by the end, she feels like a success. She aims to give a perfect show every night and is very aware of technical imperfections. If there's a sound problem, she uses inconspicuous sign language to tell her brother Michel, whose job is to take care of her and the band members.

Michel says he prefers this backstage role to performing. When he "hung up his skates" in 1988, he was relieved that the pressure was off and his fight for fame was over. Celine, he says, is much better at handling life in the spotlight. "I think all the family members are very proud of her, of course," he says. "She's the best thing in the world, and she's our sister, which is fantastic!"

One of the days he was most proud of his sister was the day their father died, and she found the strength to go out and perform right after finding out the news. "She's an artist," he says. "When she started the show, she told everybody in the audience, 'We just lost our dad. The show is going to be tough but we're going to do it.' She made a promise up there to him, 'This show is for you.' That was fantastic.

"After she finished the show, she blew a little kiss to everyone, then she came backstage and she fell down crying like a baby." Celine is quick to dismiss the praise about what a "trouper" she was—"I almost fainted backstage," she protests. It was one of the few days when she hated the responsibilities her job entails.

The weeks following his death also drew her focus from the show. Rene-Charles was particularly close to his grandfather, and Celine was very anxious about how to explain death to her son. His pediatrician advised her not to say anything until Rene-Charles asked . . . but he didn't ask.

Friends cared for Rene-Charles during the funeral, and when it was over, he took his grandmother's hand, led her to the kitchen, and set out to entertain her with his singing and dancing. Celine said it's as if he knew what was happening and wanted his grandmother to be all right.

It wasn't until the following Father's Day that he finally asked where his grandfather was. "Do you remember, every time it's your birthday we send balloons to the sky for the children who don't have any balloons? Grand-papa is with the balloons, honey," Celine told him. "You know the balloons are not coming back, so Grand-papa is not coming back." On Rene's next birthday, they released 555 orange balloons into a clear blue sky, and Rene-Charles said he was sending them to his Grand-papa.

Her father's death was the second tragedy for Celine that year. In January, she had lost her dear friend Eddy Marnay,

She wishes Eddy could see her now, to know that his worrying was for naught. Back toward the beginning of her career, Eddy had counseled Rene never to take Celine to Las Vegas. To Eddy, Vegas was where washed-up careers go to die.

"He wanted me to sing forever, and he thought if I came here, my career was going to be over," she says. "Rene kept saying, 'Vegas changed, Eddy, it's not like that anymore.'"

Eddy wasn't the only one who had reservations, though. The media was littered with gossip about the show before it ever started, full of doomsday predictions. "She'll sing only five songs, she'll never be able to do that many shows—she'll cancel all the time. She's having a helicopter transport her to the theater every night." These were the accusations Caesars president Mark Juliano says he heard during the year preceding the show's debut. And Celine, of course, heard the whispers that her career would become a joke if she played in the city of Elvis impersonators and showgirls. In usual Celine fashion, though, her determination to succeed was just amplified by the number of people who thought she was crazy for trying.

Which is not to say that there have never been problems with the show. "A New Day . . ." ran well over its original budget, and just before New Year's of 2004, Celine felt something had gone wrong. The show just didn't feel right, and she got the impression that people were avoiding her, not making eye contact with her backstage. She mentioned this new tenseness to Rene and found out that in a rush to readjust the budget, the company had just told twelve dancers that they were being laid off.

her first songwriter. "Eddy Marnay was the guardian angel of the first steps of my childhood, of my life," she says. "He wrote more than sixty songs for me. My five first albums, he wrote. He was my father in show business. He always knew how to protect me, he was a great friend with a wonderful sense of humor, and he had an answer for everything. I had never met somebody like him."

TOP: Celine with two of the most important men in her life–her father and her son. BOTTOM: Celine with father Adhemar, the last photo of them together. RIGHT: Adhemar and Therese enjoy their grandson when he visits them in Quebec.

"DO YOU REMEMBER, EVERY TIME IT'S YOUR BIRTHDAY WE SEND
BALLOONS TO THE SKY FOR THE CHILDREN WHO DON'T HAVE ANY BALLOONS?
GRAND-PAPA IS WITH THE BALLOONS, HONEY." —CELINE

To her, this was a nightmare. Those twelve dancers thought Celine knew about the decision and was ignoring it. "It's not only about twelve dancers, it's about the lives of their families, and it's about the rest of the family here who will go through the pain because they're leaving," she says. "I think we all realized it was done not to be bad—they're businessmen. They do this, but they forgot when I go on, we all share things. We all feel and sweat together. It's not about a contract. It's about a relationship, an experience, a bond."

After "two shows of hell," Celine talked to Rene on December 30th and told him that she refused to take the microphone and wish everyone a happy new year and pretend that nothing was wrong. She knew that many of the dancers had children, or had been supporting struggling families overseas with their salaries. "Do you know how many letters they wrote to me to say, 'Thank you very much. I could bring my niece here to Las Vegas to support her'? They don't know the behind-the-scenes and onstage things that are going on. Those people were chosen not only because they were talented—we can find high jumpers anywhere—but because there was an energy, a generosity among them."

She told Rene that her fondest wish would be to go to the microphone the next day and tell them that they were all staying. Only that would make it a new year to celebrate. "It's done," he said. "We'll find another way."

"When I went to bed that night, I couldn't wait for the new year," says Celine. "On the thirty-first before the show, I asked a meeting of all of them in the training room. Already ten of them were crying. They thought I was there to say goodbye to the twelve, and I said to them, 'I want all of you to stay.' It was amazing. It was a new show again. We were back. We all had a great new year."

Celine says, "I don't think this whole thing would've been worth it—the whole career, without the people I work with. Why would I attach myself with musicians from Quebec here? Because we love them all, because we grew together. It means something to me."

She doesn't understand why some artists change crews just as they're getting successful. "You're just starting to blend. You're just starting to know, like making love, you

ABOVE: Celine with the "A New Day . . ." dancers and Franco Dragone, posing for a group shot.

put your lips there. It's just becoming natural and then you let them go? What a shame."

It's a statement about her life in general. Celine says she has a very hard time letting go of people. She believes in building relationships, and it bothers her that some people can dispose of each other so easily. "I met one guy in my life and I married him, you know? It's unusual that I watch TV, but sometimes we flip through shows where it says, 'I'm fifteen years old and I don't know who the dad of my son is.' It's so sad."

ONE OF THE MOST IMPORTANT RELATIONSHIPS

Celine is building now is with herself. In her downtime now, she likes to read romances and nonfiction that tells "beautiful things about life," Rene says. This is a new phenomenon for Celine. She didn't like reading and nothing held her attention. Then, in 2003, Patrick's partner Sophie gave her a Marc Levy novel, *Et Si C'etait Vrai (If Only It Were True)* as a gift, and she couldn't put it down.

"I was in the chair singing 'Seduces Me' at night, thinking, *I can't wait to read my book*! I was thinking of the story. *If ever my fans can see through me and read my mind, if ever I forget my words, I'm going to be so ashamed of myself!* Then I read the whole book and I was very proud. I loved the story. I felt like a professional!" Celine discovered a joy in reading other books as well, and watching favorite DVDs like *Yentl* and *The Way We Were*.

"We relax," says Rene. "Sometimes we go with Rene-Charles to Chuck E. Cheese, play at bowling—he likes to go bowling. There's a place here called Mini Grand Prix where he can ride cars. He loves cars. So we'll go for a few hours with him and then maybe we'll go to a restaurant."

They have security guards with them, but the fans are mostly respectful and don't intrude. Every now and then a fan will crash a private party or sneak off with something of Celine's—even things like a half-eaten slice of cake or a water bottle she's sipped from. But there are stalkers who

---

ABOVE: Some of the many musicians who bring the performance to life. **RIGHT:** Celine working on dance moves for a "A New Day . . ."

ABOVE: The family investigates one of Rene-Charles's great interests, cars, with driver Tony Stewart and his car. **RIGHT:** In her dressing room before and after the show, Celine attends to the tasks of a star—signing posters, greeting contest winners, meeting business partners, and the like.

go farther. "I'm glad that I don't know everything, because I wouldn't be able to focus," she says. "Many times during a performance, things are happening . . . like when a guy the guards were looking for showed up and he was going to do something—they didn't tell me what, but they had to use a stun gun on him. I don't want my fans to be hurt, so I can't believe some of those people want to hurt me."

Often, the perpetrators of these more heinous acts are delusional, Celine says, believing that a song was written for them or reading meanings into her music. "Or they'll say, 'You're not wearing a bra in that picture and God is going to punish you for not wearing a bra . . . things like that. My image is pretty clean, so it's really crazy stuff."

"I feel for the fans who sleep outside," she says. "I like it because I feel I'm a happening dude, like a rock-'n'-roll star. But I don't like it on the other hand, because they don't do anything . . . they listen to your music, they tape your TV shows, come to the hotel room to see you come out so they can call, 'Celine, Celine, Celine!' It hurts to see that. What are they doing? Just grabbing on. I don't want to be part of

something that they would miss. For so many years, they follow my career, and then suddenly, what for?"

If there are people who are looking to her as a role model because they don't have positive influences in their lives, that makes her sad because all she has to offer them is a voice on the radio or TV. She can't even hug them, let alone offer any guidance or encouragement. She wants people to enjoy her music, of course, but the idea that some fans imagine a personal relationship that isn't there bothers her.

Celine knows that she opens herself up to this intense personal connection—and to criticism—by allowing the media and her fans to know so much about her private life. It's a choice she's made based on the kind of person she is and has chosen to remain. She's never dodged questions about her fertility problems, Rene's gambling (carefully budgeted with regards to both money and time!), or even the fact that Rene is the only man she's ever slept with. The more she reveals, the more fans feel they can confide in her. She's very trusting, and in her ideal world, there would be no need for gossip and secrets.

"[RENE-CHARLES] ASKS ME FOR MY MAGLITE BECAUSE HE SAW ME LIGHT WHERE SHE'S WALKING AND HE WANTS TO DO THE SAME. THE FIRST TIME HE WAS A LITTLE BIT SHY ABOUT THE NOISE AND THE LIGHTS AND THE PEOPLE. BUT NOW, HE'S WAITING FOR MOM..." —MICHEL DION

As time has gone on, though, Celine has become more assertive about separating work from their home life. Now, show business talk is allowed only in the car ride to and from the theatre; at home, they don't discuss business, and they're doing their best to give Rene-Charles a normal, if pampered, life.

"Rene-Charles thinks Caesars is Celine's hotel," says Michel. "She's the owner, because she had her picture on the wall twenty levels high. Last year he came in on his little truck almost every Friday, and after the show, he would call me and we would have to go up onstage. He wants to try the drums, percussion, dancing. And I had to give him the microphone.

"I always have a Maglite in my pocket, so one night after the show he's waiting for me stage left. He asks me for my Maglite because he saw me light where she's walking and he wants to do the same. The first time he was a little bit shy about the noise and the lights and the people. But now, he's waiting for Mom, and if she's not fast enough, he wants to go out onstage to get her."

Rene-Charles's schedule has always worked perfectly for Celine. Since birth, he's always gone to bed at two or three in the morning and awakened around 2:00 in the afternoon. So they play with him every night after the show. "He's the only four-year-old who puts his father to sleep. You think I'm joking, but Celine showed him how to tuck me in and sometimes he comes in, tucks me in, and gives me a kiss on the forehead," Rene says with a laugh.

Celine won't drop until Rene-Charles doesn't need her anymore. If he has a fever, even if it means she's up all night three nights in a row and has performances to do, she'll stay up and rock him and comfort him until the fever breaks. She hasn't yet found the limits of her strength.

———————————

ALTHOUGH CELINE MAKES IT SOUND LIKE SHE only works the nights she's on stage, that's not completely true. There are plenty of other responsibilities of being a star—there are songs to record, videos to shoot, TV appearances, commercials, interviews, awards functions, business meetings, and charity events. Even something as simple as getting her hair done is, after all, part of her job.

Before their promotional tour in October 2004, they had to fly in a hairdresser to do Celine's extensions and technicians to file her nails to perfection at her house before photo shoots. She should have been sleeping, but instead, she was entertaining these "guests." She doesn't complain, though, because she'd rather have nice hair than sleep in.

"I remember when she filmed the 'You and I' video," says Talia DeMartino. "It was a hundred and something degrees outside and none of us had slept. We were at the Colosseum the night before until four in the morning and filming started at noon. She didn't sleep and her feet were all swollen because it was hot out, but once the camera started rolling, she was walking around singing, and I thought, 'I could not do this right now.' She can just turn it on. It has a lot to do with Rene, I think, because he gives her pep talks. He doesn't allow her to give up."

Now, of course, what she wants is really up to her. She has the power to decide what to record next, who to work with, where to perform. Rarely before did she exercise her muscle to make her own career decisions, but she's speaking up more these days about her desires.

For example, Celine noticed that many fans called out to her in French during her "A New Day . . ." show, yet there were no French songs in the show. This bothered her, and she decided to add "Pour Que Tu M'aimes Encore (For You To Love Me Still)" in early 2005. The show is an ever-evolving work. When it opened, the song "A New Day Has Come" was the first song. But they pulled it out and replaced it with "Nature Boy" because "it wasn't working right," according to Dave Platel. (As of early 2005, "A New Day Has Come" has been reworked and has returned again as the show opener.) And as Celine releases albums, they plan to add a song or two from each album to the show. They're currently rehearsing some of the new songs they're planning to add in the future.

But when she talks about her return to singing, Celine gets introspective. "Sometimes I wonder why I came back.

LEFT: Rene-Charles lights his mother's way offstage during the "A New Day . . ." shows, just like his uncle Michel.

I don't know. I don't know. I don't need to," she says, voice trailing. "But I think the best is yet to come."

AS FOR HER FUTURE PLANS, SHE'D LIKE TO start a movie career. "That would be the next thing probably after this, because she can't do more than what she did," says Rene. "She played sold-out stadiums all over the world. You can't do bigger than that. This is a big production, and she's happy doing it. It's different. But after doing this, what can you do?"

Celine says she'd love to do dramas in the style of the classic black-and-white movies. "Everybody sees me in comedy, but my heart and soul don't feel like laughing so hard . . . even though I love to laugh. I think I have features for those old movies," she says.

And although she's never placed much stock in awards, she says that winning an Oscar for her acting talents would be a high she'd never come down from, because she has no right to even hope for it. Many of the best actors and actresses of our time have never won, so she says she'd know she did a heck of a great job if she could accomplish this. Maybe she'll get lucky, she suggests, and the year her movie comes out, none of the other releases will be any good!

In addition to movies, Celine says she'll keep singing, but she wants to try something different. Instead of performing pop songs in big stadiums and theaters, she wants to do scaled-down shows in smaller venues. She'd like to close the gap between the kind of music she sings in her two languages, to make the English music more like the French.

"In English, she has to perform more," Rene explains. "Well, she doesn't have to, but so far, that's what happens . . . in English, her songs are more like 'performing' songs.

ABOVE: Shooting the new music video for "You & I" in June 2004 with director Andrew McNaughton.

In French, the lyrics are very important, and she doesn't hit the high notes like she does in English all the time."

She'd like to try singing songs that are a bit darker and reminiscent of different eras—big band, jazz, soul, and even '80s hard rock. An album of Freddie Mercury's songs is on her wish list, too. "I love his pain, his experience of pain. Pain is a good thing—pain is love, as well. When you love, you hurt, and Freddie Mercury for me is pain and love. I think his soul sang much more than his vocal cords and I would love to sing him—not to be criticized, not to do better. Nobody can touch what he did, but it doesn't mean that we cannot share it. I would love to share his music and sing it for my own pleasure."

She knows, however, that the change might not be welcomed by some of her fans who've come to expect ballads from her. She's enjoyed that, but is ready for a change.

"We need to do an unplugged show," she says. "Either we do a jazz or blues album, an unplugged show with a rock-and-roll band, or a classic album with a symphony orchestra.

"That's what I'd love to do, jazz or blues. I would definitely put myself in a room and listen to the best—not trying to recreate, because the thing I want the least is to try to recreate something that's already been done perfectly. I'd want to do it with my own feeling, but I would have to put myself into the mood and listen to the best jazz or blues people out there."

Then, she says, she'd have to trust producers to tell her if her phrasing sounds right and if she's gotten the right feel of the music. "If you tell me, 'You can jump. There's water,' if I trust you, I'll jump. I'm a sponge. I grab the best of everyone, but I'm also a believer and I trust people. So if I do this blues or jazz, I'd be associated with the best people and I would jump!"

Peer Astrom would love to do blues with Celine, while Christopher Neil dreams of doing a quasi-classical album with her ("A cross between Maria Callas and Enya," he says). It seems every producer Celine has worked with has their own wish list of the types of songs they'd like to record with her, but even Rene has wishes for things he hasn't yet convinced her to do. She has played classical piano ever

since he's known her, yet she won't play a song in one of her shows. He's tried to convince her that the fans would love it if she'd just play one song, but she's too much of a perfectionist to allow it so far. She says she's not up to the level of professional concert pianists, so she doesn't want to show off her imperfections.

This is a highly different story than the one Celine tells. When I ask her about her piano-playing, she interrupts. "I don't play," she says. "I know how to play half one song, a quarter of another one. I fool around with other notes. I play three seconds on the guitar, half a song on the flute. I don't play an instrument. Whoever told you I play just *wants* me to play."

I told her she could blame her husband. "Oh, *God*," she says.

It's not the only area where their versions of events differ. She's also been known to write her own melodies—which she often doesn't even let Rene hear. He catches her singing in the shower, but her only writing credit thus far is for the melody of the song "Don't Save It All For Christmas Day." The only time she performed a song where she wrote the lyrics and the music was at Rene's daughter Anne-Marie's wedding. The two are very close, and Celine wanted to sing and record a tribute to their relationship, all the more emotional because Celine was pregnant when she sang it.

Rene would love it if she would try her hand at writing more of her own music. "That's where she's not confident. We try to encourage her," he says.

But Celine says it has nothing to do with confidence. "I think I can write good songs. I just don't have the time. Can you imagine I'm looking for a life and in the only time left I would write songs? I have a few ideas, but they're not commercial. I wrote a song in a cab in England on our way to the airport—'Drop By Drop.' I want the groove of the Beatles. I have everything in my head, the whole video, but what I want is so specific. I don't know how to tell the producer exactly what I want. He needs to feel me, to put it on the keyboard, to put it on the cello, to put in the violins.

"I don't want to do this in three days. If it takes weeks, I want to go back every day and hear the cello and say, 'I don't

A LETTER FROM CELINE

The process of creating a book that collects more than thirty years of memories is never easy. There are hundreds of notes and letters to read, thousands of photographs to inspect, and of course tens of thousands of memories and moments that come to mind—only a portion of which can fit into a book like this.

This note from Celine to you shares some of her thoughts on the creation of this special tribute to her life and career so far.

would love her to do one more album that's a crossover between pop and adult contemporary, appealing to a wide audience like *Falling Into You* did.

If she decides to do jazz, he'll support her on it, too. Of course his job is to think of the business aspects, as well, so he wants her to choose music that has the potential to hit mainstream charts—but "you never know," he says. "Look what happened with Norah Jones. She won a bunch of Grammys this year, and no one expected that. It's all about great songs."

Celine also expects to tour Europe again on a smaller scale, this time staying longer in each city instead of jetting from place to place and exhausting herself in the process. They don't have a date in mind yet because it's impossible to plan so far in advance. She'll be in Las Vegas through 2007, and after that, she hopes to take another break and have a second baby, living half-years in Florida and Montreal.

When they toured the world, the crew says they would often travel a week ahead of time or stay later so they could really get to explore the cities they were in. During winter months, they purposely booked tours in warmer climates, and sound engineer Denis says that seven or eight of them took wonderful vacations together. But Celine, he says, never got to enjoy herself like they did. She had too many other responsibilities and was never able to travel in advance or stay late. So she still feels like she hasn't seen much of the world.

"A dream of mine that I've had for a long time is to rent a big boat, like a two-hundred-footer, and book a crew," Celine says wistfully. "I want to bring some people with me: definitely my mom; my sister and Alain, who were taking care of my son; Coco and Pierre, our best friends; my best friend from Florida if she can make it with her family; Rene's children and their families; and we have three or four people we work with who cook for us and put the house together, helping us to have a quality life while we're working every day. I'd love to bring them to give them kind of a 'thank you' as well . . .

"So we would be twenty-something people on the boat. I want to fly to Europe to meet in Italy, a wonderful

ABOVE: Celine with Anne and Kel Geddes at the *Miracle* photo shoots. TOP LEFT: Celine (three and a half months pregnant) and Rene's daughter, Anne-Marie, at Anne-Marie's wedding. BOTTOM LEFT: Rene with his son Patrick, new son-in-law Marc Dupre, and son Jean-Pierre at Anne-Marie's wedding to Marc.

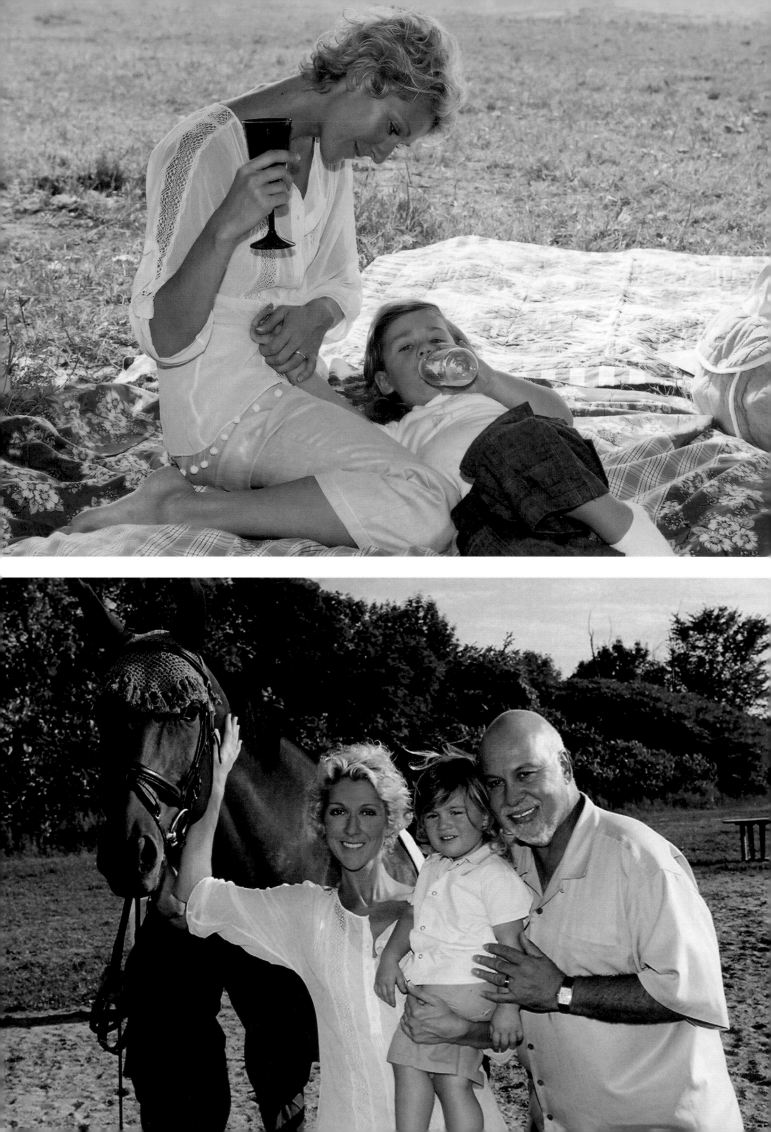

place to meet. We'd spend two weeks there, then we'd take the big boat to go to the Greek Islands. I want to drink wine, I want to have cheese, bread, and butter . . . this European style of life attracts me tremendously. I want to spend about a month, month and a half in Europe. If we decide we want to stay three or four more days in Saint Tropez, there's no schedule. That would be my gift to us after Vegas."

She'd love to sunbathe topless without worrying about paparazzi snapping pictures, and she'd love to have a little time off from the image people expect of her. "I want to be my whole self. I want to be grounded," she says. "When you become so successful, you become a prisoner of that success. The water is so hot, it's like you're swirling around in a Jacuzzi and you can't get out. I'm not saying it's not good—it's pretty comfortable to be in a hot Jacuzzi, but sometimes you need to cool down, and I surely don't know how and I surely wonder if it's possible."

Part of the reason she sometimes feels like a prisoner is that she knows there are certain expectations that she set up herself. She's the sweet woman who sings lullabies and love songs, who never complains, never makes a scene, lives a fairytale life. It's not that it feels false, but neither is it the whole story. "Sometimes it's even too much for me and I want to come out of my own shell," she says.

Coming out of her shell would mean speaking up more instead of saying things like, "Oh, I know it's part of the business. I don't mind." It would mean dressing however she wanted—sexier or like a punk rocker if she felt like it. It would mean not worrying if a fan overheard her say a swear word if she stubbed her toe. She can do all this in front of the people who know her well, which is why it sounds so attractive to cruise around the ocean with these close friends and family members.

After this trip, she and Rene would fly to New York and go to the fertility clinic to try to have another baby. Celine thinks she'd be too stressed and fatigued if she tried to get pregnant right after her Las Vegas show, so she wants a couple of months to unwind and loosen her grip on the "good girl" lifestyle.

"I do everything by the book. I want to go out, I want to drink, I want to dance, I want to make love and eat too much. I want to jump in the ocean, jump upside down, and not worry about losing a baby. That's why I want to have this time first. And I don't want to bring any luggage—I want to shop for everything there. They'll ask, 'Do you have anything to declare?' and I will say, 'Sure . . . everything! I have my whole life to declare.'"

She'd want to give her next baby the same amount of attention she was able to give Rene-Charles, so she wouldn't plan to work for at least a year. When she was pregnant with Rene-Charles, she had begun language lessons so she could record an album in Spanish. Unfortunately, when Las Vegas came calling, that fell by the wayside. Maybe if she takes another "maternity leave," she'll have time to take up where she left off and feel ready to do the Spanish album she's always wanted to do.

Many members of Celine's team have followed her lead and started families of their own in these past few years. "We all have families now, which we couldn't afford before, because we were on the road," says Patrick Angelil. "I was out for two months, back one month, out for two weeks . . . it was hard to have a family life on those circumstances. Then we stopped here, which was Celine's dream . . . the same dream shared by many of us. It was an opportunity to have a stable life for once."

But professionally, Patrick misses touring. His job was more exciting when he had more logistical planning to take care of, and he smiles when I ask if he wants to tour again after Vegas. "I'm waiting for that. I have a family now, but Celine has a family, too, so it won't be the same. We won't go for a year with short breaks in between. I think we would go for three months and come back, or stay longer in smaller cities. I'll bring my family with me."

CELINE OFTEN ASKS HERSELF WHAT WOULD happen if her career ended tomorrow. Could she live without the helpers who cook and clean for her? Absolutely, she's decided; in fact, it's a little unnerving to stumble out of bed and have to face the people who are preparing your breakfast and making your bed before you're even out of the room. She dreams of the day when her life slows down enough for her to handle these tasks herself. She'd like to learn her mother's recipes, drive her son to school, plant her own flower garden. Even if she does love the people who work for her, it's hard to feel like her house is all her own.

CELINE HOPES THAT AFTER SHE RETIRES, PEOPLE will remember her not just as a singer, but as an entertainer and as a person. Unlike when she was a teenager, she now loves it when people call out to her during her performances and she gets to engage in a dialogue from stage.

"I don't want people to think that I'm doing the show and I can't get out of the show or I would lose my whole self. I'm in control of myself. I like to do different things that aren't part of the show, because they see my personality, and

I care for that very much. An entertainer is somebody who can take control in different situations and talk to people," she says. "Sometimes I want to show the side that I'm focused and serious, but sometimes I love to fall with them. Every night is a different night."

Her talent, she believes, was given to her. Of course she had to work on it and still does, but she won't feel it's any great accomplishment if all people remember about her is the voice she was born with. What matters to her more is that people get to know what she's made of—her humor, spirit, morals, love, passions, attitude, strength, weakness, loyalty—and who she's chosen to be.

What many people around her say they've learned from her is that you can be a big star with all the adoration and luxuries a person could want and remain a nice human being. It seems Celine is immune to her own hype; never does she imagine that her talent makes her any more worthy or interesting than anyone else she meets.

Maybe this is what it is about Celine that makes people want to open up to her. As we sat on the floor and chatted through the wee hours of the morning, I soon felt tremendously comfortable in her presence, able to tell her things that only my closest friends knew. Warmth begets warmth, and it's not hard to see why so many people feel a connection with her. There's a child-like honesty here, an openness you'd never expect from someone who's lived in the public eye. Above all, there's a love that she gives freely to anyone open to receiving it.

Together, we looked through old photos and letters from fans and staff members. She recognizes the ones that have meant the most to her just by glancing at the handwriting, and has fragments of them memorized. Celine feels privileged that fans want to share their lives with her. Sometimes she feels that she learns more from them than they do from her, and it makes her happy when people tell her that her drive or her music has inspired them to pursue their own paths.

"Life is so precious and it goes so fast," she says. "People should not wait too long to make the best of themselves, to make a difference, or to fulfill their dreams."

RIGHT: Celine's priorities are now clear to her: family first and profession second.

DISCOGRAPHY

LA VOIX DU BON DIEU
(1981, Les Disques Super
Etoiles inc.)

CELINE DION CHANTE NOEL
(1981, Les Disques
Super Etoiles inc.)

TELLEMENT J'AI D'AMOUR
(1982, Les Productions
TBS inc.)

LES CHEMINS DE MA MAISON
(1983, Les Productions
TBS inc.)

CHANTS ET CONTES DE NOEL
(1983, Les Productions TBS inc.)

LES PLUS GRANDS SUCCES
(1984, Les Productions TBS inc.)

MELANIE (1984, Les Productions
TBS inc.)

C'EST POUR TOI (1985,
Les Productions TBS inc.)

CELINE DION EN CONCERT
(1985, Les Productions
TBS inc.)

LES CHANSONS EN OR
(1986, Les productions
TBS inc.)

INCOGNITO (1987, CBS Disques
Canada Ltee)

UNISON (1990, CBS Music
Products, Inc.)

DION CHANTE PLAMONDON
(1991, Sony Musique Inc.)

CELINE DION (1992, Sony Music
Canada Inc.)

THE COLOUR OF MY LOVE
(1993, Sony Music Entertainment
(Canada) Inc.)

CELINE DION A L'OLYMPIA
(1994, Sony Music Entertainment
(Canada) Inc.)

D'EUX (1995, Sony Music
Entertainment (Canada) Inc.)

FALLING INTO YOU
(1996, Sony Music Entertainment
(Canada) Inc.)

LIVE A PARIS (1996, Sony Music
Entertainment (Canada) Inc.)

LET'S TALK ABOUT LOVE
(1997, Sony Music Entertainment
(Canada) Inc.)

S'IL SUFFISAIT D'AIMER
(1998, Sony Music Entertainment
(Canada) Inc.)

THESE ARE SPECIAL TIMES
(1998, Sony Music
Entertainment (Canada) Inc.)

AU COEUR DU STADE (1999,
Sony Music Entertainment
(Canada) Inc.)

ALL THE WAY... A DECADE
OF SONG (1999, Sony Music
Entertainment (Canada) Inc.)

THE COLLECTOR'S SERIES
VOLUME ONE (2000,
Sony Music Entertainment
(Canada) Inc.)

A NEW DAY HAS COME
(2002, Sony Music
Entertainment (Canada) Inc.)

ONE HEART (2003, Sony Music
Entertainment (Canada) Inc.)

1 FILLE & 4 TYPES (2003,
Sony Music Entertainment
(Canada) Inc.)

A NEW DAY... LIVE IN LAS
VEGAS (2004, Sony Music
Entertainment (Canada) Inc.)

MIRACLE (2004, Sony Music
Entertainment (Canada) Inc.)

ACKNOWLEDGMENTS

MANY, MANY THANKS TO ADRIENNE WILEY FOR entrusting me with this book and her encouragement and editorial insight along the way.

Everyone involved with CDA and Feeling Productions treated me like family and made this a wonderful experience for me. Celine, never would I have dreamed that I'd get to say this, but thank you for being my friend. You're an unforgettable person and I love you. Your couch can sneak-attack me anytime. Rene, thank you for your genuine warmth and for the great honor you gave me by sharing your stories with me.

Dave Platel and Talia DeMartino, thank you for coordinating with me and helping at every turn. Michel Dion, you're everything a big brother should be. Patrick Angelil, thanks for your great insights and kindness. Suzanne Gingue, your caring heart inspires me.

But perhaps I owe the biggest thanks to the fans who have followed the making of this book from day one. Those who run fan Web sites, particularly Val and Bruno of Celine-Community.com; Vic and Bellamy of CelineChannel.com; Thom of CelineDionWeb.com; Yuri of CelineDreams.com; and Alfonso of CelineManiacs.com, were so supportive and helpful to my research. And the members of online forums told me their stories, shared the questions they wanted me to ask, and even offered up suggestions for titles and cover art. Thanks in particular to the German and Dutch fan groups, as well as Thomas, Elisa, Andre, Ashley, Darryl, "The SCF Slayers" (especially Haylica and Anna), Ben, Duchess, Marisa, Jillian, Tal, Tatiana, Del, Lisa, Tativale, Ben, and Jon-Paul Cunningham.

Thank you to my readers at AbsoluteWrite.com for the constant stream of encouragement and advice. Cheryl Ryshpan, thank you for sharing your memories with me and offering to show me around Montreal!

And of course, thank you to Anthony, Lori, Mark, Paul, Lisa, and the Policastros for letting me know I'll never walk—or fly—alone.

becker&mayer! would like to extend a special thanks to Sylvie Beauregard and her team of assistants—Stephane Rivest, Veronique Martin, Therese Beaupre, and Marie-France Allie—for all the hours and hours of research to gather materials for this project. Thanks also to Lina Attisano, Paul Farberman, and Mia Dumont for their many important contributions. Thanks, too, to Steve Gerstman, licensing agent for Five Star Feeling/CDA Productions, for his help with this project. Thanks to Dorothy O'Brien and Andrews McMeel for their vision for this book.

ABOUT THE AUTHOR

JENNA GLATZER IS THE EDITOR IN CHIEF OF AbsoluteWrite.com (the most popular on-line magazine for writers) and the author of fourteen books. Among her latest are *Fear Is No Longer My Reality* with Jamie Blyth of *The Bachelorette* (McGraw-Hill, 2005) and *Make a Real Living as a Freelance Writer* (Nomad Press, 2004). She's also a contributing editor at *Writer's Digest* and has written hundreds of magazine articles and essays for anthologies such as the *Chicken Soup for the Soul* and *A Cup of Comfort* series. She and her husband live in New York. Her official website is www.jennaglatzer.com.

TRANSLATIONS

PAGE 36

Attention: Madame Hyest

To the Director of Departmental Manpower,

We are producing at the Olympia Celine Dion, who will be performing in Patrick Sebastien's shows from November 6th through December 9th 1984.

We would like to have a work permit for her and her musician.

You will find, attached, all the necessary formalities. Thanks in advance,

Yours truly,

Rene Angelil

P.S. Thank you for sending the work permits directly to the Olympia.

PAGE 96: SPECIAL AMBASSADOR TO UNESCO, SPEECH

Notes for an address made by the Minister of Culture and Communications Madame Agnes Maltais Honoring Celine Dion with a Certificate for "UNESCO's Artist for Peace" Montreal, December 15th 1999 at 3:00 pm The reading is the authentic text

Madame Dion, Monsieur Angelil, Madame Sheila Copps (Minister of Canadian Heritage), Mister Michel Agnaief (President of the Canadian Commission for UNESCO), Madame Ndeye Fall (UNESCO representative), Distinguished guests,

Ladies and gentlemen,

The new millennium is the perfect moment to erase all past errors, lovelessness, and indifference toward the suffering of others. It gives us a chance to start writing a new history.

We are at page one. All of humanity wishes to redefine itself with new consciences, new solidarities.

As Minister of Culture and Communications,

I believe in the power of art, its ability to heal and to elevate the human soul. Whether an artist, a minister, or a simple citizen, we have not only the power, but the duty to interfere to create a better world around us.

Mr. Kofi Annan, Secretary to the United Nations, said that "peace is in our hands." As of now, it is also in the voice of Celine Dion, strong and flawless.

It is the first time a Quebec artist has been granted the title of "UNESCO's Artist for Peace," and I am particularly glad that this honor was offered to Celine Dion, a young native of Charlemagne, Quebec. It is no accident that she was born right after Expo 67, in a different Quebec, a stronger Quebec totally open to the world.

Her loyalty to her roots has never faltered. Celine Dion is a warm and spontaneous young woman. She has always spoken highly of her country, of her large family, and of all the true values of love and generosity attached to her past, and the main source of her inspiration.

Millions of Quebeckers are behind her, watching her go, proud of what she has achieved and loving her for what she is: an international megastar deeply attached to her roots. She is a true Quebecoise, profoundly human.

The famous French sociologist Edgar Morin once said: "There is compassion inside every man, but it doesn't last." Celine Dion's compassion is everlasting. Barely in her thirties, she has been a benefactor of the Canadian Foundation for Cystic Fibrosis, a disease that killed her niece Karine in 1993, for seventeen years.

For her farewell concert on December 31st, she will donate one million dollars to this Foundation. Celine Dion is very aware of the suffering of others.

Her world renown and the true affection that people from all over the planet show her give even more meaning to each of her actions. That is probably the greatest and most interesting part of all her fame.

If only one song could bring peace to the entire world,

I am sure that Celine Dion would have sung it already.
It would have been a natural gesture for her, since she has
already sung of the power of love in many of her songs.

She sang, "If being in love was enough . . . if love
itself was enough . . ." I think Celine Dion knows that
loving alone is never enough.

I am convinced that she still hopes that this could
be possible, one day, although she has "nothing but a song
to face a drum." Carrying the strong love she received
from her parents, her thirteen brothers and sisters,
and her husband, she continues spreading a message of
hope around the world.

Peace comes from beauty. It starts with people
getting together, starting a dialogue to find the true
meaning of life. Artists like Celine Dion give us that.

Peace is a precious gift, a treasure we would like to
share with every human being.

Dear Celine, now "Artist for Peace," I wish you and
Rene a peaceful life and a wonderful sabbatical year.
Let's hope, selfishly, that this absence will not last long.
You still have so much to share with us.

PAGE 96: SPECIAL AMBASSADOR TO UNESCO, LETTER

Madame Dion,

You seemed to enjoy the tribute I recently gave about
you on behalf of the Quebec government.

Maybe you would like to know that the speech I
delivered was written by an author, an artist, and a friend,
Mrs. Helene Pedneault.

I had asked her to write my speech mainly because
she was part of a musical theatre company called Les
Folles Alliees, which I was part of in the '80s, singing
your song "D'amour Ou D'amitie" as our tour hymn . . .

Agnes Maltais
Minister of Culture and Communications
P. S. All my best wishes for the new millennium.

PAGE 120: CELINE AND RENE WEDDING PROGRAM

Musical Menu

Morency Quartet: *Denise Lupien, violin;
Olga Ranzenhofer, violin; Francine Lupien-Bang, viola;
Christopher Best, cello*

Jazz Piano Trio: *Tilden Webb, piano; Eric Lagace, bass;
Peter C. Magadini, percussion. Guest musicians:
Stephane Allard, violin; Jean-Pierre Zanella, sax;
Mohammad Abdul Al-Khabyyr, trombone*

21 Strings Orchestra: *Under the musical direction
of Hun Bang*

David Foster: *Directing a twenty-string orchestra;
Warren Wiebe, singer*

Harry Birkens's Strolling Trio: *Viennese and
Gypsy music; Harry Birkens, accordion;
Ireneusz Bogajewiez, violin; Jean Pellerin, bass*

Perry Carmen and his Orchestra: *Karine, singer*

Gastronomical Menu

Duo of salmon tartare, five-pepper seasoning;
Quenelle of caviar
Chardonnay, Fortant de France
Brome Lake duck confit radiotore; sorrel coulis
*Chardonnay, Fortant de France, or
Cabernet Sauvignon, Fortant de
France collection*
A duet of goat cheese with thyme flowers on a
bed of fresh leaves
*Cabernet Sauvignon, Fortant de
France collection*
Trio of fruit sorbets
Signature Croquembouche, presented as a
giant Christmas tree
Lanson Rosé champagne
Coffee and liqueurs
Executive chef: Abdesattar Zilouni
Pastry chef: Maryan Krawezak

IMAGE CREDITS

Many of the photographs featured in this book were taken by family, friends, employees, and associates of Celine and Rene at the various social and business events they have attended around the world. These pictures are part of the Feeling Productions Archives. Feeling Productions would like to thank the following individuals for these photo contriubutions:

FRONT COVER PHOTOGRAPH: Andre Rau.
FROM THE ANGELIL PERSONAL COLLECTION: 7, 76 (top left), 99, 101, 109, 112, 117, 121 (bottom) 128, 129, 130, 131, 133 (both), 135 (all), 137 (top), 138, 139 (both), 141, 142 (both), 147, 155, 158 (top), 168 (top), 169, 176. Album, p. 136: My first picture, Tucking in Rene-Charles, Feeding doll, Snowmobile, Bowling, Elvis, Hawaii, Sleeping in Papa's arms. Announcement, p. 136: Rene-Charles alone (both).

COURTESY OF L'ACTUALITE (PIQUEMAL/GAMMA): 42.
PHOTOGRAPHS BY PETER ARNELL: 5, 102, 103.
PHOTOGRAPHS BY DANIEL AUCLAIR/LES PUBLICATIONS TVA: 115, 116 (right).
COURTESY OF BILLBOARD: 54.
PHOTOGRAPHS BY GEORGE BODNAR: 2, 72, 73, 83, 121 (top), 151, 157, 160, 166, 170.
PHOTOGRAPH BY LINDA BOUCHER: 52.
PHOTOGRAPHS BY MANON BOYER: 182 (both).
PHOTOGRAPH BY MICHAEL CAULFIELD/WIREIMAGES: 106.
PHOTOGRAPHS BY LAURENT CAYLA: 89, 99 (bottom), 107, 108, 111, 113, 122, 125, 126, 127, 128 (bottom, both), 144, 168 (bottom), 184 (both), 185. Album, p. 136: With Therese, Bob the Builder.
COURTESY OF CBS PRODUCTIONS: 86.
COURTESY OF CBS (SONY MUSIC)/BERNARD BOURBONNAIS: 46.
PHOTOGRAPH BY CLAUDE GASSIAN: 81.
PHOTOGRAPHS BY RICHARD GAUTHIER: 187. Album, p. 136: Golfing.
COURTESY OF THE COLLECTION OF ANNE GEDDES: 183.
PHOTOGRAPHS BY ANNE GEDDES: Announcement, p. 136: With Celine, With Celine and Rene.
PHOTOGRAPH BY MARK GLATZER: 189.
COURTESY OF THE GRAMMY AWARDS, 1993: 61.
COURTESY OF THE GOVERNMENT OF CANADA, PRIME MINISTER'S OFFICE: 105.

COURTESY OF HARPO, INC.: 154 (bottom).
PHOTOGRAPH BY KENT KALLBERG: 55.
PHOTOGRAPH BY GILLES LAFRANCE: 123.
PHOTOGRAPHS BY GILLES LAFRANCE/LE JOURNAL DE MONTREAL: 150, 158 (bottom), 159, 175.
PHOTOGRAPH BY JEAN F. LEBLANC, COURTESY OF L'ADISQ: 82.
PHOTOGRAPH BY MARC LOSTRACCO: 178.
PHOTOGRAPHS BY ARTURO MARI, COURTESY OF THE VATICAN: 34 (all), 35.
COURTESY OF MARTIN PHOTOGRAPHY: 53.
PHOTOGRAPH BY FRANK MIRAGLIA: 156.
PHOTOGRAPH BY ROBERT MORA: 164.
PHOTOGRAPH BY ROBERT MORA AND TOMASZ ROSSA: 149.
PHOTOGRAPHS BY PARAMOUNT PICTURES/ BERLINER STUDIO: 76 (bottom, both).
PHOTOGRAPH BY PARK PLACE ENTERTAINMENT: 153 (top).
COURTESY OF LUCIANO PAVAROTTI: 94 (top).
PHOTOGRAPHS BY JEAN-BERNARD POREE: 37, 65.
PHOTOGRAPHS BY TOMASZ ROSSA: 9, 154 (top), 165, 172 (all), 173, 181.
COURTESY OF SONY MUSIC FRANCE: 69.
PHOTOGRAPHS BY DIMO SAFARI: 57 (top), 74, 79, 98, 116 (left), 119, 125 (bottom left).
PHOTOGRAPHS BY GERALD SCHACHMES: 132, 134.
PHOTOGRAPH BY ALAN SILFEN: 50.
PHOTOGRAPHS BY DAVID L. SMITH: 174 (all).
PHOTOGRAPH BY DENISE TRUSCELLO: 152.
PHOTOGRAPH BY DENISE TRUSCELLO/WIREIMAGES: 94 (bottom).

PHOTOGRAPH PROVIDED BY ANDRE FORGET/AFP/ GETTY IMAGES: 92.